Scorpio
24 October – 22 November

First published in Great Britain 2010
by Harlequin Mills & Boon Limited,
Eton House, 18-24 Paradise Road, Richmond, Surrey TW9 1SR

Copyright © Dadhichi Toth 2007, 2008, 2009, 2010 & 2011

ISBN: 978 0 263 87385 6

Typeset at Midland Typesetters Australia

Harlequin Mills & Boon policy is to use papers that are natural, renewable and recyclable products and made from wood grown in sustainable forests. The logging and manufacturing processes conform to the legal environmental regulations of the country of origin.

Printed and bound in Spain
by Litografia Rosés S.A., Barcelona

About
Dadhichi

Dadhichi is one of Australia's foremost astrologers. He has the ability to draw from complex astrological theory to provide clear, easily understandable advice and insights for people who want to know what their future might hold.

In the 27 years that Dadhichi has been practising astrology, face reading and other esoteric studies, he has conducted over 9,500 consultations. His clients include celebrities, political and diplomatic figures, and media and corporate identities from all over the world.

Dadhichi's unique blend of astrology and face reading helps people fulfil their true potential. His extensive experience practising western astrology is complemented by his research into the theory and practice of eastern systems of astrology.

Dadhichi features in numerous newspapers and magazines and he also appears regularly on many of Australia's leading television and radio networks, where many of his political and world-wide forecasts have proved uncannily accurate.

His website www.astrology.com.au is now one of the top ten online Australian lifestyle sites and, in conjunction with www.facereader.com, www.soulconnector.com and www.psychjuice.com, they attract over half a million visitors monthly. The websites offer a wide variety of features, helpful information and personal services.

Dedicated to The Light of Intuition

Sri V. Krishnaswamy—mentor and friend

With thanks to Julie, Joram, Isaac and Janelle

Welcome from
Dadhichi

Dear Friend,

Welcome to your astrological forecast for 2011! I've spent considerable time preparing these insights for you. My goal is to give you an overview of your sign and I hope you can use my simple suggestions to steer you in the right direction.

I am often asked by my clients to help them understand their true path and what they are supposed to be doing in life. This is a complex task; however, astrology can assist with finding some answers. In this book I attempt to reveal those unique character traits that define who you are. With a greater self-understanding, you can effectively begin *to live who you are* rather than wondering about *what you should do*. Identity is the key!

Knowing when the best opportunities in your life are likely to appear is the other benefit of astrology, based on planetary transits and forecasting. The latter part of the book deals with what is *likely* to happen on a yearly, monthly and daily basis. By coupling this section with the last chapter, an effective planner, you can conduct your business, relationships and personal affairs in ways that yield maximum benefits for you.

Along with your self-knowledge, there are two other key attitudes you must carry with you: *trust* and *courage*. Unless you're prepared to take a gamble in life, earnestly and fearlessly, you'll stay stuck in the same place, never really growing or progressing. At some point you have to take a step forward. When you synchronise yourself with the powerful talents found in your Sun sign, you'll begin to understand what your mission in life will be. This is the true purpose and use of astrology.

So I invite you to gear up for an exciting fifteen months! Don't shrink back from life, even if at times some of the forecasts seem a little daunting. Don't forget that humans are always at their best when the going gets tough. The difficult planetary transits are merely invitations to bring out the best in yourself, while the favourable planetary cycles are seasons for enjoying the benefits that karma has in store for you.

Remain positive, expect the best, and see the beauty in everyone and everything. Remember the words of a great teacher: 'The world is as you see it.' In other words, life will reflect back to you only what you are willing to see.

I trust the coming fifteen months will grant you wonderful success, health, love and happiness. May the light of the Sun, the Moon and all of the stars fill your heart with joy and satisfaction.

Your Astrologer,

Dadhichi Toth

Contents

The Scorpio Identity

A happy man is too satisfied with the present to dwell too much on the future.

— Albert Einstein

Scorpio: A Snapshot

Key Characteristics

Secretive, passionate, determined, tactless, loyal, hardworking and inflexible

Compatible Star Signs

Scorpio, Taurus, Capricorn, Cancer, Pisces

Key Life Phrase

I will

Life Goals

To transform yourself into the best you can become

Platinum Assets

Ability to overcome at all costs, sexual attractiveness
and
willpower

Zodiac Totems

The scorpion, the lizard, the phoenix

Zodiac Symbol

♏

Zodiac Facts

Eighth sign of the zodiac; fixed, fertile, feminine, moist

3

Element

Water

Famous Scorpios

Hillary Rodham Clinton, Bill Gates, Joaquin Phoenix, Bjork, Julia Roberts, Richard Dreyfuss, Winona Ryder, Indira Gandhi, Carl Sagan, Joni Mitchell, Demi Moore, Leonardo DiCaprio, Larry Flynt, Prince Charles of Windsor, Bill Bryson, Martin Scorsese, Boris Becker, Calvin Klein, Jodie Foster, Bill Wyman, K.D. Lang and Pablo Picasso

Scorpio: Your profile

Scorpio is a fixed water or icy sign, born under the eighth sign of the zodiac. You have received some pretty bad press, Scorpio, and are probably the most misunderstood sign. You show a cool, aloof exterior to the world but underneath you have a scorching and passionate nature. Both Mars (aggression) and Pluto (magnetic forces) rule the sign of Scorpio, so the battling energy of Mars and the hidden depths of Pluto will influence you.

The old saying goes still waters run deep and in this way you could likewise have the power to wear away rocks, or at least reshape them, given enough time. Unfortunately what people don't understand, they will fear, and this is the case with you.

You need approval and the emotional part of your nature is the most significant area of your life, even though you don't often verbalise it. Although you demand a lot of others, you are no less demanding on yourself and, when you give your heart to someone, and they in turn give theirs to you, you are the most loyal person. You absolutely adore the idea of love and this is a challenge that constantly excites you.

Your home is indeed your castle and you like it tidy, orderly and a place to which you can retreat. The home is jealously guarded because this is your territory and reflects your personality; your likes and dislikes.

Tenacity is one of your strengths and when you decide to do something it takes a lot to talk you out of the project (even if someone has the gall to try). You give your all and will push the boundaries as far as needs be to achieve what you want in your business or personal lives.

You are sensual by nature and, with your alluring magnetism, draw people to you from all walks of life, whether social or professional. You have a powerful and magnetic aura and cannot walk into a crowded room without being noticed, even before you say or do anything. People are attracted to you and, because you are the strong, silent type, you possess something that makes it near impossible for others to ignore you.

You are well aware of your power to manipulate anyone who comes within your orb, and you love it! This secret and enigmatic power of yours is probably your greatest strength. It's a well-known astrological fact that Scorpio's eyes can hypnotise, and this is a physical trait you possess. People may even say to you, 'you have the most amazing eyes'. Your eyes are the perfect tool for communication and express the whole range of your complex and changeable emotional states.

You can be single-minded and this may be mistaken for being insensitive to the needs of others. However, this is only because you want to be the best at what you do and there are no half measures with a Scorpio, be it your friendships, love, family life or profession. You aim to be the best and will not allow anything to stand in the way of your success.

Determination is yet another of your key words, but you are quite prepared to share your successes with the people you take care of such as family and friends. Any obstacle or challenge that comes your way, whether naturally occurring or placed there by competitors, will only serve to make you prove you cannot be stopped once you have made up your mind. If someone tries to corner you or put you in a difficult situation, they'd better be prepared for when your competitive nature comes to the fore.

You have a ruthless streak in your character and won't give in until the job is done and the enemy totally vanquished, even if you have to wait patiently until the appropriate time to seek revenge. Pity the poor unlucky recipient of that vengeance when you unleash it!

You are not afraid of the dark, even though you aspire to the light. All pleasure becomes part of your domain and your sensual appetites need to be fulfilled. You give 100 per cent and expect that percentage to be returned, and it usually is.

It is interesting that Scorpios can be equally as successful as saints or sinners and will stop at nothing to achieve their aims, whichever way they decide to go.

Scorpio has three totems that describe its nature—the scorpion, the lizard and the phoenix. The scorpion is the most vengeful and dangerous aspect of your nature and if you're operating on that level you'll constantly seek to hurt others with your power. The lizard represents the class of Scorpios who hide from life and never quite achieve the full measure of their power. They often seek self-destructive outlets such as drugs or even criminal activities to fulfil their obsessive needs. If you aspire to the best of the Scorpio's three characters, then you'll be represented by the phoenix, which appears rising up out of the ashes. Generally we find Scorpios aspire more to the latter quality.

Your appearance will be well proportioned, with a muscular, strong body, a broad face and a majestic, commanding look. As already mentioned, your eyes are your strongest physical characteristic and, because the enigmatic planet Pluto rules a Scorpio, you're also fiery and aggressive. You are a tireless worker and generally achieve great success after the middle part of your life.

Three classes of Scorpio

If as a Scorpio you were born between the 24th of October and the 2nd of November, you are a charismatic and rather sensual character who possesses many noble aspirations. You are a pleasure seeker who will make enjoyment a focal point of your life. In your youth you may have spent time exploring the sexual part of your personality.

If you were born between the 3rd and the 11th of November, you are an idealistic and spiritual type of Scorpio. You have a strong leaning towards understanding the meaning of life and delving deeply into the true nature of your being. Philosophy is one of the cornerstones of your personality.

Being born between the 12th and the 22nd of November, you are one of the more sensitive types of Scorpio because you are partly affected by the Moon. Your key challenge is to bring greater control to your emotions and not be swayed by the events that come your way in life. You have a compassionate streak as well.

Scorpio role model: Carl Sagan

Scorpios are known for their desire to explore the unknown. This is perfectly seen in one American astronomer, astrophysicist and author, who popularised astronomy Carl Sagan worked long and hard pursuing his own path to make a name for himself through his researches into the astronomical realms.

Like him, you too have the ability to explore the universe and discover the truth.

Scorpio: The light side

People are drawn to you, Scorpio, because you are the seducer of the zodiac. You have a sophisticated sexual magnetism that will not be ignored. Your body, and in particular your eyes, will make the world look at you, and many will desire you.

Friends know you can keep a secret and they will confide in you, as they know whatever they tell you will go no further. It is almost as if your aura has a healing quality and they can draw on your energy. Your mere presence, even with few words, will tend to alleviate their problems and they will feel much better when in your company.

You can be generous to a fault in some ways but very possessive in others. It is a little quirky that if someone doesn't make undue demands on you, you'll give them the world. Scorpio, you have a humanitarian side to your nature where you like to lend a hand, lift the spirits of others, and to you it is the natural thing to do.

You can make others feel great and this is one of your best assets. None can surpass Scorpio's technique and ability in the sexual, romantic arena. You're a born lover and your electric sexuality will bring much pleasure to many people throughout your life.

You are intuitive and can use your natural-born

Scorpio instincts to come up with quick solutions without too much intellectual effort. This is second nature to you, but surprising to others.

Scorpio: The shadow side

Scorpio, you need to make allowances for the fact that not everyone has the same high level of energy as you do. If they don't, it doesn't mean that they are not passionate, loving or serious about their relationships or what they do. Don't equate a lukewarm reaction or half-hearted attitude from others in work or play as a weakness.

People are just basically different and have many ways of showing their love and commitment. You can be possessive of those people close to you, especially family and lovers, although you are loyal and protective once you have made a commitment.

Loyalty is high on your list of 'must haves' and, if anyone crosses you, you will not forget it. You can be described as vengeful and are prone to mete out maximum damage if you feel the disloyalty or harm is serious enough. It would be wise to keep in mind that if the punishment must fit the crime, be very sure of what the crime actually is. Sometimes you will just have to let bygones be bygones and accept that not everyone is going to live their life by your high standards but simply by their own.

The sexual side of your nature can cause you health problems and also emotional rifts with lovers if you need excessive bouts of sexual play and your partner does not have the same level of sensuality as you. Try to moderate this part of your nature and, rather than bottling up your feelings and exploding later, share your feelings at the time in a much calmer way.

Scorpio woman

The Scorpio woman can be far too intense for the average male and could even turn them off when their demands and expectations become too high. However, you are proud of the fact that you are uncompromising in virtually everything you attempt, especially love.

Your expectations in love are that you want at least an equal, but not greater, return for the amount of time and emotional investment you make in a relationship. Your motto seems to be 'all or nothing at all' and this can be quite daunting for some prospective suitors. Grey is not a colour you are familiar with: it is black and white all the way for the Scorpio gal.

You expect 100 per cent commitment from your partner, just as you are prepared to give the same, and when you do give your heart to another, no sacrifice is too great. Body, mind and soul are what's on offer from you, Scorpio, and you would find it difficult, if not impossible, to present anything else. You would even be prepared to give up everything for that ideal.

Some of your peers envy your confidence and unless they get to know you well they may mistake this self-belief for arrogance and pride, when in fact this is not the case at all. You are simply a strong character and are not afraid to let the whole world know it.

Although you have sexual magnetism in abundance, unlike many women you do not rely on this to achieve goals in life. You prefer to be accepted for your talents and hard work, not your sexuality. You dance in time to your own tune.

Any form of indecision or weakness in a prospective partner or friend is a real turn-off for the Scorpio woman, who needs someone with at least equal power to her own. Telling people what you really think is not difficult for you; however, you are extremely sincere when you deal with others at every level in your life.

Honesty does not scare you in the least, either given or received, and this is one of your greatest traits. This straightforward honesty, however, could attract enemies in life, but so be it, Scorpio. This is just the way you are and the odd enemy or two throughout life will not really make that much of an impression on you, anyway, so just accept that this is part of your package.

You have great intuition and can sniff out the truth in any remark, not matter how well veiled it may be. Your suspicious nature will often cause you some difficulties in your most personal relationships and, if your passions are stirred on any topic, you'll argue the point relentlessly until you win.

You find disloyalty most repugnant. Being ruled by the planets Mars and Pluto, you will express your love fully to whomever you give your heart. You understand the art of love and are extremely passionate and sensual.

You enjoy nurturing and nourishing your young children and are very dedicated to giving them a good life. A clean and tidy house is what you desire and it matters not whether it is a modest-sized home or a mansion; it will receive the same amount of care and attention. You will guard your home and your family jealously. You'll always look after your partner, giving them all the pleasures they desire throughout your life together.

You hate to be possessed, even though you, Scorpio, are possessive; so this part of your nature can become a bit of a balancing act for you.

Scorpio man

You can be misunderstood by those around you because your intensity is often mistaken for repressed anger or other negative emotions. You can be seen as extreme in nature, but actually you are simply being serious about what you do and often don't choose to explain this to those around you. If you are the strong, silent type who broods and keeps your emotions under wraps, this will add to your mystery as a Scorpio man. However, if you spend just a little more time allowing others to get to know you, they will find a deep, mysterious, loyal and loving human being.

Your eyes are magnetic, mesmerising and penetrating, and it is this single feature that most represents your Scorpio nature. Your eyes reflect your depth, the passion of your mind and heart, and people will often comment on this. You are quick to read others, judge them, and are usually spot on with your well-developed intuitive powers.

Other non-Scorpios may need the opinions of many people before they come to the same conclusion that you seem to make in the blink of an eye, much to their amazement. You are a natural-born psychologist and understand humans much better than most of the other star signs in the zodiac. Many Scorpios are interested in psychic and occult topics and some even go on to become professional astrologers or clairvoyants due to this highly refined ability. Misuse of this power, however, could see a fall from spiritual grace that otherwise could be easily obtained.

Your ego is powerful and potential partners readily accept that you have an almost in-built need to prove your sexual abilities. However, you need to go beyond the purely possessive instincts of lust and reach a deeper, perhaps spiritual awareness of what love actually is. It's not a bad idea to sow your wild oats early in life and get that need out of your system.

Many Scorpio males are addicted to sex, money and power, with the three often overlapping. After a sufficient period of exploitation of your sexual nature, your higher Scorpio nature will redirect your energies positively. Later on, the phoenix part of your Scorpio character will allow you to soar to an elevated stratosphere of life without these emotional constraints.

Work can become all-consuming for the Scorpio male, making it an almost obsessive daily routine and some may even become workaholics, or at least border on it. The Scorpio male does nothing by half measure; it is all, or nothing at all. Your colleagues often envy your energy level and you work long and hard, allowing nothing to get in the way of your ambitions.

You even appear to be so self-absorbed that you are insensitive to the needs of others around you and brush them aside as if what they have to say, no matter how important, is not nearly as significant as your own agenda. This self-centredness and indifference should not be allowed to flow over into your family life, especially with your children. Spend quality time with them and work to live, not live to work.

Scorpio child

The Scorpio child is an old soul in a young body, and one look into their eyes will tell you exactly that. They absorb information at an astonishing rate and have a deep understanding of the world way before they can even walk. Scorpio children are competitive beyond their years; they love to be the best at what they attempt and being number one is where they aspire to be.

Scorpio children love to be around adults, be involved in the social and family environment that they are so much a part of. They are curious, adventurous and love nothing better than exploring and conquering their environment, answering for themselves many questions to which they just have to have an answer.

They have dreams of climbing mountains, being a great explorer, going where no one has gone before and see no reason why they can't do it, either. Inventiveness and other discoveries should be considered when buying the Scorpio child a gift, or it will just stay in the corner and gather dust.

The young Scorpio girl will be happy cooking, trying out new things to eat and be at mum's elbow in the kitchen. Boys, being extremely competitive, will do well in sports that require tenacity and stamina. They need to win at all costs and come out on top of any sporting activity they take on.

The Scorpio child makes an excellent friend, is loyal and focused, but does need to be the centre of attention in their peer group. If being chosen as the leader is not forthcoming they will simply move onto another group who will grant them their rightful position (they think) as number one.

They are quick and intuitive learners and should be encouraged in subjects that naturally interest them; otherwise they will become bored and just work out the easiest way from A to B because it is not worth their effort to do anything else.

Throughout their teen years it may be difficult to keep them on the straight and narrow because they have a natural predisposition towards the darker sides of life, including drugs, alcohol and other nefarious activities.

A child born under the sign of Scorpio can be secretive, but must be respected for needing time alone and having their own space. In this way they will develop more quickly in a positive way and love you all the more for it.

Romance, love and marriage

The eighth sign of the zodiac is ruled by Scorpio and says it all about their attitudes to love, sex and marriage. A Scorpio has a heightened awareness of their sexuality and anyone who chooses this zodiac sign as a partner can be assured of their loyalty and sensuality.

Love is an intensely passionate and enduring emotion to a Scorpio which may be directed towards only one person. Many of the ambitions and actions of a Scorpio are inspired by this love.

Sex is an important element of a relationship with a Scorpio and, when making love, this is an expression of all the pent-up passion that is hidden in this most magnetic of personalities. Scorpio is actually the sign of the zodiac that exhibits the greatest interest in sexual matters and, as in other aspects of their life, the Scorpio partner is both inventive and single-minded.

The Scorpio lover feels they have every right to be the dominant partner in a relationship. Secrecy is part of the Scorpio personality, although they will be responsive and demonstrative, too, so there could be a degree of challenge in there as well. A Scorpio partner can be jealous and possessive, but this doesn't always sit well with other star-sign partners. Taurus is a good match on this level because they can anchor you and secure you to their earthiness, somehow balancing the extremes of your nature.

You know what you want from people, Scorpio, and you don't see any point in beating about the bush and wasting time when you are quite clear about the direction you must take. The people you come in contact with will instantly sense this about you. However, if you are too heavy handed, this could cause others of less strength to walk away from a relationship of such intensity.

Scorpios do not enter into a relationship lightly and are only faithful when deeply in love, preferring to play the field until they meet their ideal match. It is only then that they will give themselves totally and completely.

Be warned that the best way to send a Scorpio off into an affair with another person is to relegate sex to the bottom of your list of priorities. To a Scorpio, this will immediately send out signals of rejection and this is not a path you want to tread, believe me! Be prepared for a very rocky time if you reject a Scorpio partner. A rejected Scorpio is unlikely to forgive, and will never forget, the hurt. They will want to exact revenge.

Scorpios have a somewhat dark and broody personality and are sometimes very difficult for their partners to fathom. You certainly don't put all your cards on the table and hold them close to your chest, only letting your partner see what you want them to see.

When emotionally stressed a Scorpio can shut down, making it very difficult if not impossible for their partner to figure out what is going on inside them. Consider that some of your own insecurities may be at the bottom of your desire to dominate and be completely in control of the relationship.

Scorpio men and women are wonderful homemakers, possibly the best in the zodiac. They pride themselves on the quality of their homes, take great care of their families and will jealously guard their abodes.

You have extremely strong principles about how your home should be organised; its neatness and orderliness are uppermost in your mind. However, your disciplinarian attitudes could take over and disrupt the very tranquillity you are trying to achieve, so be less heavy handed and try to show the softer, gentler side of your personality to maintain a peaceful family home.

Scorpios are rarely demonstrative in public but the one they love will certainly know how they feel when the bedroom door is closed. This is where Scorpio shines, showing tenderness, imagination and sensuality in their lovemaking.

Although Scorpio does not put a lot of faith in romance, and may not show their feelings or emotions to others too readily, they expect their partner to be aware of how lucky they are to be a part of their world. Plenty of admiration for them will go a long way with a Scorpio.

Health, wellbeing and diet

Scorpios are strong, robust people with a high level of vitality, good health and a long life. Many workaholics are born under the sign of Scorpio, but with Mars being one of your ruling planets, your ailments usually pass quite quickly and your recuperative powers are amazing.

Scorpio primarily rules the reproductive system and the sexual and excretory systems of the body. It's important to keep these parts of your system functioning well, with a lot of fresh water in your diet. Aries rules a further sector of health for Scorpios and this involves the head, eyes and brain, so overwork can affect these parts of your body.

Being very physical in nature, it is important to do plenty of stretching before strenuous exercise and this will help avoid stresses and strains in your muscles, ligaments and tendons.

You really don't like your health being a bit below par because it slows you down, but if you take care of the wonderful engine that is your body, you should be able to maintain optimum health for much of your life. Your mind also can play a part in determining the quality of your health, so be aware that such illnesses as depression can leave a Scorpio feeling depleted.

For a Scorpio, overeating and mixing too many different types of foods is a one-way trip to reduced health and a lowered vitality. Even though your taste buds crave hot, fiery and exotic dishes, these should be eaten in moderation because they can have an irritating effect on your digestive system.

One of your ruling planets Mars is also fast moving, so health-wise it is in your best interests to slow down when you are eating. Chew your food thoroughly and try and eat your meals in a relaxed atmosphere. Peace and quiet, soothing music and allowing ample time for enjoying your meals are ways that your system will cope better with your food intake.

For a workaholic Scorpio, skipping meals or getting fast-food takeaway to eat at your desk while on the phone, is a recipe for a very upset stomach. Remember, Scorpio, your body is your temple and should be treated with care and respect.

To help your body cope with the speed with which you do things and the intensity of your nature, try to augment your diet with pumpkin, carrot, red beans and lentils, all of which are a source of high protein energy and antioxidants for you.

Work

Mars, being one of your ruling planets, can direct you towards independent but high-pressure work, so the military or police service would fit you well. However, with the vitality of the Sun ruling your professional destiny, you will shine brightly no matter what career you choose.

Scorpios are excellent at healing professions and particularly those that involve the intuitive part of your nature. Investigation and research are interesting to Scorpios and therefore you'd make an excellent analyst or strategist, especially given your hard-working nature and dedication to a job.

You love power, so other professions that may suit you well are insurance, banking, investing, market analysing, or as an astrologer or psychic adviser.

Jupiter holds sway over your finances and the speculative sector of your horoscope, so the stock market may be of interest to you and you should do well through investments of this nature.

You are extremely hard working, whether as an employer or employee, and loyalty and effort are characteristics of your sign. You are self-motivated, imaginative, a problem solver and you know how to use your intuition to improve your workplace and the systems being used, sometimes much to the amazement of your colleagues.

Key to karma, spirituality and emotional balance

For you, Scorpio, your spiritual goal could be to learn the meaning of selfless love. Your desire to control others, without giving them enough scope for their own expression, needs to be watched. This could cause an imbalance in your relationships, especially those based on emotion.

You can certainly speak your mind; but remember that, just as equally, others have the right to do so as well. Scorpios are very high-powered and imaginative people and are sometimes intolerant of those around them who are not as quick on the uptake. Give others the freedom to express themselves, albeit slightly slower than you do, Scorpio, and all in the garden will be rosy.

Try to relax by finding outlets for all that pent-up energy that you amass during the course of a day. A hobby that anchors you while sparking your interest and providing you with intellectual stimulation will go a long way towards keeping that balance in your life, which is so important for you.

Your lucky days

Your luckiest days are Mondays, Tuesdays, Thursdays and Sundays.

Your lucky numbers

Remember that the forecasts given later in the book

will help you optimise your chances of winning. Your lucky numbers are:

9, 18, 27, 36, 45, 54

3, 12, 21, 30, 48, 57

2, 11, 20, 29, 38, 47, 56

Your destiny years

Your most important years are 9, 18, 27, 36, 45, 54, 63, 72 and 81.

Star Sign Compatibility

Any idiot can face a crisis; it's day-to-day living that wears you out.

— Anton Chekhov

Romantic compatibility

How compatible are you with your current partner, lover or friend? Did you know that astrology can reveal a whole new level of understanding between people simply by looking at their star sign and that of their partner? In this chapter I'd like to share some special insights that will help you better appreciate your strengths and challenges using Sun sign compatibility.

The Sun reflects your drive, willpower and personality. The essential qualities of two star signs blend like two pure colours, producing an entirely new colour. Relationships, similarly, produce their own emotional colours when two people interact. The following is a general guide to your romantic prospects with others and how, by knowing the astrological 'colour' of each other, the art of love can help you create a masterpiece.

When reading the following I ask you to remember that no two star signs are ever *totally* incompatible. With effort and compromise, even the most 'difficult' astrological matches can work. Don't close your mind to the full range of life's possibilities! Learning about each other and ourselves is the most important facet of astrology.

Each star sign combination is followed by the

27

elements of those star signs and the results of their combining. For instance, Aries is a fire sign and Aquarius is an air sign, and this combination produces a lot of 'hot air'. Air feeds fire and fire warms air. In fact, fire requires air. However, not all air and fire combinations work. I have included information about the different birth periods within each star sign and this will throw even more light on your prospects for a fulfilling love life with any star sign you choose.

Good luck in your search for love, and may the stars shine upon you in 2011!

Compatibility quick-reference guide

Each of the twelve star signs has a greater or lesser affinity with one another. The quick-reference guide will show you who's hot and who's not so hot as far as your relationships are concerned.

SCORPIO + ARIES

Water + Fire = Steam

Scorpio, strap yourself in for quite a ride if you choose to team up with an Aries. A roller-coaster has nothing on this combination and, just as there will be peaks, so too will there be troughs. We have two very strong-willed individuals in this pairing and the combination of water and fire makes for a very steamy affair, giving this partnership quite a sizzle.

You will each sense the passionate and sexual side of the other's personality and there will be a

Quick-reference guide: Horoscope compatibility between signs (percentage)

	Aries	Taurus	Gemini	Cancer	Leo	Virgo	Libra	Scorpio	Sagittarius	Capricorn	Aquarius	Pisces
Aries	60	65	65	65	90	45	70	80	90	50	55	65
Taurus	60	70	70	80	70	90	75	85	50	95	80	85
Gemini	70	70	75	60	80	75	90	60	75	50	90	85
Cancer	65	80	60	75	70	75	60	95	55	45	70	50
Leo	90	70	80	70	85	75	65	75	95	45	70	90
Virgo	45	90	75	75	75	70	80	85	70	95	50	75
Libra	70	75	90	60	65	80	80	85	80	85	95	70
Scorpio	80	85	60	95	75	85	85	90	80	65	60	50
Sagittarius	90	50	75	55	95	70	80	85	85	55	60	95
Capricorn	50	95	50	45	45	95	85	65	55	85	70	75
Aquarius	55	80	90	70	70	50	95	60	60	70	80	85
Pisces	65	85	50	90	75	70	50	95	75	85	55	80

natural affinity between you. After the raging and clashing of wills as you both try to assert your superiority, there can always be a sweet time for the kiss-and-make-up sessions—and what a hot time that can be between these two star signs!

However, there could be a battle of wills when you first start out together because here power is the name of the game. How you use this power will determine the amount of joy and happiness you can extract from this relationship.

You both have very unique personalities with individual underlying strengths, therefore compromise will be the cornerstone of making it or breaking it. Scorpio will excite the hot-headed Aries and Aries will stimulate Scorpio's desire to explore the possibilities of life with them.

Because Scorpio is the sexual zone for Aries, this is the part of your relationship that will dominate. Your Sun sign is ruled by the passionate Mars and Pluto. This combination can mean that at times you are somewhat icy and controlling, which often makes it difficult for the average Aries to understand what is really going on.

In the domestic arena you may have conflicts. You, Scorpio, are secretive and like your home to be your haven, neat and orderly, whereas Aries on the other hand wants the house to be the centre of excitement, people coming and going, and generally being party central. Aries will find it hard to negotiate on this issue and may not understand why there is any problem with this sort of lifestyle. But it most certainly will be a problem—for you.

Arians born between the 21st and the 30th of March make a fiery and dynamic combination with you, Scorpio. They will not be too happy about your emotional control games, but if you can give them the space they need, then the good sexual relationship you experience will more than make up for these other areas.

With those born between the 31st of March and the 10th of April, you will get a run for your money when they attempt to dominate you. This will be even more exasperating if you are working together in professional activities. In fact, it could be a disastrous combination if you get involved with them because Scorpio definitely doesn't like submitting to another.

The Arians best suited to you are those born between the 11th and the 20th of April because they have Jupiter and Sagittarius co-ruling them. You have very strong emotional and karmic connections with any Aries born during this period.

SCORPIO + TAURUS
Water + Earth = Mud

Well, here we have the opposites attract scenario, according to the astrological charts. In Taurus, Scorpio can learn to recognise the talents of other people and appreciate their value, learning along the way how to value their own talents more realistically. Scorpio, being more self-critical than most other signs of the zodiac, often reproaches him or herself in the company of this sign.

Many Scorpios have been attracted and attached to their opposite sign of Taurus. Mars and Pluto give Scorpio their powerful drive and magnetic appeal and, given that Taurus has the ruling planets of Mars and Venus, there is an undeniable connection between you.

You will find Taurus dynamic and overpowering. Even though they may not say or do too much on your first meeting, you will undoubtedly feel their passion and excitement. A Scorpio woman may seem more subtle than her male counterpart, happily accepting the subordinate role; however, this is only so she can achieve her ambition in the end.

Scorpio is a fixed and watery, or icy, sign. With a Taurus, with their element of earth, you won't be quite so fluid. There can be a conflict of interests between these two star signs because you, Scorpio, can be cold and inflexible and Taurus has an earthy stubbornness. There may be situations where you individually dig in your heels and won't budge and this could drive you both crazy at times. Each of you needs to respect the other's viewpoint and try to avoid a head-on confrontation where nobody wins.

Sex gives you the opportunity to express your love and, because Taurus is naturally touchy-feely by nature, they will be flattered by the attention. Taurus, however, does need you to express the more affectionate and sensitive side of your nature, not just the sex, for them to feel that the relationship will last. You can help Taurus explore the untapped part of their nature in which love and sensuality can reach a pinnacle and in turn they will show you how to get in touch with the softer side of your personality.

Money, power and control can be real sticking points in this combination and can get in the way of developing a deeper love for each other. Don't let these issues drive the relationship or become a major testing ground for your feelings towards each other.

Those Taureans born between the 21st and the 29th of April will suit you quite well and a true love match, even marriage opportunities, can be established with this group.

You could also be attracted to Taureans born between the 30th of April and the 10th of May, but this is more likely to be a platonic relationship rather than a love match. These Taureans are more suited to social activities and it may feel uncomfortable taking a friendship with this group to the next level.

Business arrangements could be a real success with those born between the 11th and the 21st of May. But before getting too involved with them you will have to sort out and understand their financial needs. They have a real need for security and, once this side of the relationship is accepted, the emotional and sexual aspects will do quite well.

SCORPIO + GEMINI

Water + Air = Rain

The communication styles of Scorpio and Gemini are quite different. You, Scorpio, prefer depth and a radically transformative approach to discussion, while Gemini is light-hearted, frivolous and likes to keep things quite breezy. As a couple you should prepare yourselves for some pretty intense times due to this difference in style, because it may not sit well with you, Scorpio.

To you, Gemini may seem a little fluffy and lightweight because they tend to talk about a multitude of things whereas you're not as content just to sit and have an idle chat. Your style is to explore deeply into a topic and Gemini may find this too difficult to deal with all the time. Compromise will be the key word to make this combination a happy union.

The ruling planets of Scorpio are Pluto, Mars and Mercury, with Pluto and Mars bringing out the intense side of your personality. However, Gemini's ruler Mercury doesn't easily fit with yours and this may ultimately create some uneasiness in the friendship. But if you show patience with Gemini, they may be prepared to learn that your probing and relentless mind can actually reveal the deeper side of their intelligence, too, and raise them to a greater level of personal growth.

Likewise, Scorpio can also benefit from this combination if you can lighten up a bit and let

Gemini show you how to have a more easygoing attitude to life. Geminis like humour and lots of fun, so go along with them and see what's on offer in a relationship with them.

Gemini may feel that you are trying to dominate and control their emotions, but you will still find considerable sexual satisfaction between the sheets. You will surprise Gemini with your depth of feelings and passion and they will respond. This will draw Gemini closer to you, even though they are less intense than you are, Scorpio.

The relationship may not survive your possessive and jealous nature Scorpio because Gemini is socially more inquisitive and adaptable than you are. For this combination to succeed there will need to be a great deal of adjustment from both of you in order to strike a happy balance.

Although there typically isn't a strong enough bond to keep a relationship going between you, with the right focus and combination of your forces, it can be a win–win situation in business or finance.

There's something about the group of Geminis born between the 2nd and the 12th of June that brings out your generous nature and you may find yourself spending your hard-earned cash on them, and willingly, too. A professional association would be better with this group of Geminis, and you may even meet them through a co-worker or business function. This is a great combination for getting things done, having the blend of Scorpio determination and Gemini flair.

Geminis born between the 22nd of May and the 1st of June will produce a relationship full of wit, charm and laughter, but it may not deliver the passion you expect and desire, Scorpio. This group may find it difficult to express their feelings and a lot of patience will be required from you for this match to succeed.

There could be an interesting journey in store for you with those Geminis born between the 13th and the 21st of June. They are partly ruled by Uranus and Aquarius, are unconventional, and like to do things that have a certain amount of shock value attached to them. Therefore, they could create opportunities to let the less conservative side of your personality emerge.

SCORPIO + CANCER
Water + Water = Deluge

When two people are born under the same element, in this case water, generally they feel comfortable and attracted to each other. You are both sensitive, emotional and caring, but have different ways of expressing love.

Scorpio, your love is demanding and asks more of Cancer than they can possibly give. Cancer may feel that they are doing as much as they can for you emotionally, only to realise that, somehow, you feel it is never enough.

You also need to learn to curb your desire to dominate and push sensitive Cancer away with your often unrealistic demands, on both practical and emotional levels. Cancer needs to be made to feel that you value their part in the relationship, and this will give them a much-needed boost to their input.

Cancer can handle your jealousy and possessiveness much better than most other signs of the zodiac because they are adaptable and can adjust to your Scorpio willpower, which you tend to use to gain what you want, when you want it.

Although Scorpio and Cancer are elementally well suited, both being water signs, sexually they are different. The sensual and sexual aspects of a relationship are what drives a Scorpio and they frequently need much more passion in their lives than Cancer does. However, what Cancer needs is love and bonding, not just raw sex, before they can express the passion that you're after, Scorpio.

Cancers need a 'cause' to which they can dedicate themselves emotionally, and initially this may unnerve you, but at the same time endear them to you. Your strong and silent exterior can be off-putting to some signs, but Cancer can navigate the direct channel to your heart and soul. You can have a long and loving relationship with them, but to do so, you must open up your heart.

Those Cancers born between the 22nd of June and the 3rd of July are highly sensitive but may seem a little weak in your estimation. However, they are still capable of bringing out the deepest emotional aspects of your character. It is quite possible that you could work together in humanitarian situations where you are helping other people, but you mustn't let this overshadow the relationship and dominate the direction of your lives.

Cancerians born between the 4th and the 13th of July have a strong Scorpio affinity and this will satisfy your complex needs. Your magnetic and sexual energies will be apparent from the outset and your water elements will naturally seek out and feel at ease with each other.

The group of Cancers born between the 14th and the 23rd of July are ruled by the Moon and you can expect to have lots of fun times with them. They are the original party animal and, if you want to kick up your heels and have fun, this is the group you will want to be with.

SCORPIO + LEO
Water + Fire = Steam

This is certainly a combination where the best ego wins. You both have very strong wills and well-developed egos, but you each need to feel respected by the other if this is going to be a successful relationship. Stubborn and inflexible are words that cover both of you, but your icy and brittle nature, Scorpio, will slowly melt under the beneficent rays of Leo's warmth. Your patience will be required if Leo is able to break through your emotional barriers and enjoy the sensitive side of your nature.

You, Scorpio, for the most part, are an emotional, sensual and intense personality, and this is exactly the energy that attracts Leo to you. The combination of these two star signs creates a powerful and emotional relationship.

Both Scorpio and Leo are extremely romantic and loyal, so they tend to mate for life, even when there are challenges to the innermost circle of their relationship; for example, Bill and Hillary Clinton. They both have a desire for power and this is probably the mainstay of their deepest relationship because, in their case, 'united they stand, but divided they fall'. Through thick and thin, they have endured storms in their public and private lives and emerged as a very powerful couple.

Scorpio's fascination with such things as death and the afterlife may unnerve Leo a little, because some of these topics may seem too deep psychologically for them. They would prefer that Scorpio backs off for a while from time to time so they can absorb what's on offer and get their head around what Scorpio is trying to get across to them.

Leo may not at first seem fond of Scorpio's interests, but because they have a tremendous respect for a deeply analytical mind, they will want to prove their worth to you in psychological realms. Once Leo shows you, Scorpio, that they are up to the task of philosophical investigation and deep enquiry, this will intrigue and fascinate you, therefore drawing a lot of respect for Leo.

Whereas Leo is outwardly happy to exert their dominance and prowess while strutting the stage of life, so to speak, Scorpio is not quite as up-front.

They like to have a card up their sleeve just in case something untoward and unexpected comes along and they will still covet that token of power they love so well. Leo has a showy, dramatic flair and this is not the way of Scorpio, who is quieter, deeper and more analytical.

Leos born between the 24th of July and the 4th of August have a very powerful sense of self and will be quite opinionated. This will get on your nerves, Scorpio, and the relationship could become a tug of war about who submits to whom.

Those Leos born between the 5th and the 14th of August sometimes need to exaggerate and drama-tise things far more than Scorpio would prefer.

You are probably better suited to a long-term partnership with Leos born between the 15th and the 23rd of August. Your temperaments are far more compatible than either of the other two groups.

SCORPIO + VIRGO
Water + Earth = Mud

The most basic elements of nature are earth and water, and this perfectly sums up the compat-ibility between your water sign of Scorpio and the earth sign of Virgo. Plants, trees and shrubs cannot survive without both of these elements, and are what gives our world its beauty.

A happy and comfortable life can certainly be achieved between Scorpio and Virgo because they are naturally attracted to each other's elements.

By pooling their financial, mental and emotional resources, a secure and fulfilling relationship can be sustained.

However, at the opposite end of the spectrum is that couple who seem to be constantly at odds with each other. They may marry, stay together for life, but may never be quite fulfilled. The common denominator with this combination of Scorpio and Virgo is that you are both very demanding people in your own way.

Generally there is a good connection between the signs of Scorpio and Virgo because your star sign happens to be the sign of communication to Virgo. Also, Virgo happens to be in the area of friendship in the zodiac and offers lifelong fulfilment for Scorpio. So, whichever way you look at it, there are some pretty promising aspects for you as a couple. Two very different planets happen to rule you and a deeper appreciation of each other's motives will help enormously in solving any of the problems or differences that you encounter.

Pluto, your ruling planet, is dominant and challenging in the most confrontational way, whereas Virgo has a more prudent mind and prefers to do battle intellectually in a courteous and unassuming way. Virgo may feel that your insensitive attitude and blunt manner shows a lack of respect and ignores their basic emotional needs. Virgo will irritate you and possibly even completely frustrate you with their overly logical analysis of every minor issue that comes along. You will need to lighten up,

Scorpio, if you are to feel more confident in your relationship with Virgo.

However, this combination has all the hallmarks of becoming a really great relationship on a practical level and also in the bedroom. Financially Virgo can offer you the support you require where investments and practical security are concerned, and the two of you can work towards financial stability, bringing prosperity and a sense of being settled. Scorpio and Virgo can create a mutual support system that offers you more than the basic emotional and romantic fulfilment you seek.

The group of Virgos born between the 3rd and the 12th of September may offer gains and losses in your financial relationship with them. The old saying of never mix business with pleasure rings true with these Virgos.

Virgos born between the 24th of August and the 2nd of September are quite the opposite in nature to you because Mercury co-rules them. Do you really want to take this relationship to the next level?

Those Virgos born between the 13th and the 23rd of September are ideally suited to you; you'll feel naturally attracted to this group and will want a bright future with them.

SCORPIO + LIBRA
Water + Air = Rain

Mars, Pluto and Venus combine to create a dynamic and passionate love match between Scorpio and Libra.

These are the ruling planets for both of your star signs and they are the typical male–female planets that represent love throughout history and astrological folklore.

There will be a few striking differences to overcome in the partnership, even though you will be extremely attracted to the sensual and sensitive Libran and they in turn to your very ardent and hot-blooded Scorpio temperament.

Libra prefers a far more open-ended social or romantic arrangement and your possessive and sometimes demanding attitude, Scorpio, will be far too constrictive for delicate Libra to handle. At some point your jealous streak will be something that Libra will find difficult to come to terms with and you could be in for a rude awakening. Libra will have to dig deep into their reserves of diplomacy to get around your controlling and inflexible nature.

Libra, an air sign, will stimulate you and challenge your thinking by presenting you with new avenues of discussion. You have a deep perception of life and are intrigued by the mystery of human nature and life in general. This also fascinates Libra and draws them nearer to you on a level that other star signs may not even be able to imagine.

Scorpio, your silent treatment will frustrate Libra no end as they try to extract information and explanations from you, so you need to let your partner know not to hold their breath while you decide what to divulge to them and what to keep secret. Otherwise they could expire from a lack of oxygen.

In a long-term relationship there could be an opportunity for making a lot of money together if you support each other in a material sense, but communication and intellectual understanding will be a necessary component for this match to work.

Librans born between the 24th of September and the 3rd of October could burden your finances, unless rules and boundaries about shared money are clearly outlined at the outset. Loans or other borrowings should be avoided with this group to remove conflict and differences of opinion.

You'll have a hard time remaining grounded with Librans born between the 4th and 13th of October because they are indecisive about most matters that you would normally consider easily solved. Libra likes to explore every opportunity and avenue, whereas you, Scorpio, are more likely to act upon your decisions quickly and firmly.

An excellent relationship can be had with Librans born between the 14th and the 23rd of October. They will offer you companionship, support and can come up with wonderful, timely advice. This will be a good match.

SCORPIO + SCORPIO
Water + Water = Deluge

Well, Scorpio people, is it heaven or hell you're after? This match may not be what other star signs would find idyllic because it has all the elements of power play, tremendous upheavals and intense mood swings due to your basic inflexibilities. However, depending on how much unconditional love you can bring to this relationship, these problems may be overcome.

The first and immediate attraction between Scorpio and Scorpio is your unbridled passion and in many cases this desirability actually deepens your love for each other. Very quickly you will realise that there is a possibility of a lifelong commitment in this combination.

Another Scorpio can share your secrets because they feel that they truly understand you from the inside out and there is a certain synchronicity with them. They are able to help you without even bringing words into the solution because their very presence is comforting to you.

You are extremely possessive, jealous and suspicious of each other because of this deep love. You demand loyalty and a completely one on one relationship, which in due course could stifle the relationship because it will be so intense. Being able to trust your partner is a lesson that must be learned if this combination is to survive and, if neither of you is willing to grant a certain amount of personal freedom to the other, the relationship will be snuffed out like a candle that needs oxygen to keep the flame alight. Working on your loyalty to each other is far more productive than giving your suspicions a run, wouldn't you agree?

In choosing another Scorpio, one of your own star sign, the group born between the 24th of

October and the 2nd of November are instantly attracted to you. Once you become involved, you may find yourselves feeling as though you are almost two halves of the same person; such is the similarity in your personalities. Your sexual appeal will also be a winner in this matching.

Scorpios born between the 13th and the 22nd of November will offer a softer and more emotional relationship because the Moon and Cancer filter through these Scorpios' personalities and tend to bring out the very emotional side of your nature. If it's a family life you're after, then these Scorpios will be ideal for you because they are soft, caring and very family orientated individuals.

The best combination with another Scorpio is probably those born between the 3rd and the 12th of November, being partly ruled by Neptune and Pisces. They're idealistic and believe that the most important thing in life is unconditional love. They will provide you with almost everything you need to feel as though you are in the perfect relationship.

SCORPIO + SAGITTARIUS
Water + Fire = Steam

The ruling planets of Scorpio and Sagittarius are very friendly. Scorpio is ruled by Mars and Pluto, and Sagittarius by Jupiter, which is a formidable combination that usually indicates expansion, optimism and great success. With both of you having a positive view of life, you are able to achieve great things.

Sagittarius is outgoing, sometimes even audacious, and initially you will be wary of this larger-than-life character. However, this combination can work if Sagittarius remains mindful of the fact that you, Scorpio, are more serious in your attitude. Sagittarius can reflect a deeper and more considerate aspect of their personalities, even though others would be of the opinion they are generally quite blunt.

The archer has a love of freedom and likes to be here, there and everywhere; but don't be fooled that they are not thinkers. Sagittarius, in fact, is a sign of philosophy and they will connect well with your interest in the occult and psychic arts as well. This will be a common ground for you to indulge in many discussions and you can both learn new things. Psychic hunches and intuitive responses are not unknown with this partnership, and it will be a continual source of amazement to you both how you can, at times, finish each other's sentences.

These two star signs are a unique combination and, with the energy that you exude, heads will turn in a room, or even eyes will roll from those around you. A combining of these two star signs can be the start of an explosive relationship; exaggerated and excessive. This partnership could burn out if Sagittarius doesn't stick to some of the basic emotional and mental ground rules that you lay down, Scorpio. However, Sagittarius is able to draw you out of your brooding moods and show you what a good time is really all about.

Sagittarius can add another dimension to your experience, Scorpio, and you must learn to relax a little and just go along for the ride, enjoying the lighter and more optimistic sides of life. Travel is certainly an area where you can experience new and exciting things, and nobody likes to take a trip more than a Sagittarian. They probably always have their bags semi-packed in case an opportunity presents itself.

Exploring different cultures, seeing the way the rest of the world lives and loves, will definitely increase your knowledge and will give you a taste of freedom and variety. Sagittarians are natural givers and therefore your love life can be exciting, too, even though it may be one-sided until you learn to trust them, Scorpio.

Your business partnerships and any working arrangements you have with Sagittarians born between the 23rd of November and the 1st of December also work well and stimulate the financial aspects of your relationship.

Sagittarians born between the 2nd and the 11th of December will feel very connected to you because Mars is the common planetary ruler for both of you and resonates well.

Ego clashes are likely to arise with Sagittarians born between the 12th and the 22nd of December because these individuals tend to be more wilful and egocentric than the typical Sagittarian. You'll need to engage your best diplomatic skills to survive a friendship with them.

SCORPIO + CAPRICORN
Water + Earth = Mud

Scorpio and Capricorn can be compatible, although your ruling planets are not the best of friends. In astrological terms, Scorpio falls right in the centre of the area of friendship of Capricorn and you will quickly grow to feel a strong sense of kinship with this Saturn-ruled star sign and be comfortable with each other. Capricorn instinctively feels you have their best interests at heart, although they are sometimes as cautious and mistrusting as yourself.

Capricorn doesn't like being taken out of their comfort zone. This is essential for their sense of stability and security and so your own commonsense will make them feel very at ease with you. You will be drawn to their sensible attitude on a practical level, but also their emotional and sexual attitudes as well. Although you are two self-absorbed and complicated personalities, you can meet in the bedroom, where your sexual attitudes and mutual magnetism will set up quite a frisson between you.

A safe haven will be provided by both of you for your family, where you will give unstintingly of your love for your children and each other. Your family will be well nurtured and will not want for any of the world's material things.

Scorpio and Capricorn are industrious, hard-working and committed to achieving mutual goals with equal determination, though you aren't necessarily motivated by the same desires. You, Scorpio, are less motivated by money than emotional passion, but you do like the power and leverage money can bring with it. Capricorn is more concerned with what money can buy and the comforts in life it will afford.

With the combination of these two attitudes, this is a formidable partnership that will bring tremendous material wealth and power. However, balance is necessary if you two are to work and play together, since power conflicts are inevitable with this pairing.

Your sexual compatibility can be at odds due to the very different nature of your ruling planets. Scorpio, yours is an outgoing planet in terms of sexual expression and Capricorn, with a far more reserved attitude, may initially feel threatened and mistrusting of Scorpio's overwhelming sexual enthusiasm. Capricorn needs time to mature into expressing the sexual side of their nature, which will eventually be satisfying to you both, but only if you, Scorpio, are prepared to give them the time they need to get to know you.

Relationships with Capricorns born anywhere between the 23rd of December and the 1st of January may be too stifling for you, Scorpio. This group has the double influence of Saturn, which makes them very conservative and less likely to share their inner feelings with you until they really get to know you.

Capricorns born between the 2nd and the 10th of January are the ones that are best suited to you because they have passionate Venus influencing them, and you may even wonder if they are Capricorns at all due to their sensual affection.

There are two very different sides to the personality of those Capricorns born between the 11th and the 20th of January. One side is very outgoing while the other is secretive, which is not unlike you, Scorpio!

SCORPIO + AQUARIUS

Water + Air = Rain

Inflexibility is the name of the game here, where both of you have spines like steel and won't bend or yield on any issue, idea or opinion. You may well wonder if there is any possibility of a relationship between these two signs of the zodiac, let alone a long-term commitment or even something more permanent, like marriage.

Your ideas about life are so fixed and will probably become more so as you age. If you do choose, against all the odds, to go into a relationship with an Aquarian, both of you will need to deal with these issues sooner rather than later.

Scorpio and Aquarius are fixed or immovable signs of the zodiac and both are determined individuals who stick to finishing what they begin. This could be called stubbornness by some, or it could be seen as sticking to your guns when you know you are right. The positive side of this is that, once a project is begun, it will no doubt be completed and you are not afraid of the ups and downs along the challenging road of life in the meantime. It is essential in a relationship to be of the mindset that what you commence should have longevity.

Scorpio and Aquarius, although both stubborn and inflexible, are different in their essential characters. Scorpio has a more emotional and personal agenda, whereas Aquarius tends to hold its ground on matters of ideology. Aquarius will try to coerce you to be part of the 21st century in ideas and ideologies, but you, Scorpio, are far more interested in down-to-earth matters.

Aquarians are very progressive in their ideas and will want to involve everyone around them in their far-out philosophies. This will probably not work for you, and you are likely to dig in your heels and hold your ground when you feel their approach is not totally appropriate.

When this sort of situation arises you will need to use your powers of communication to find some compromise outside of your personal bias. During this process you will learn much about each other and remove any intolerance that there may be in the initial stages of a partnership.

Communication is very important in another part of a relationship between Scorpio and Aquarius, and that is in the bedroom. If Scorpio wants to explore the sensual and sexual depths of Aquarius to bring out their passionate side, preferring, themselves, to express feelings in a raw and unbridled form, Aquarius will just have to learn that too much talking is a turn off.

Aquarians born between the 21st and the 30th of January are rather erratic in nature and shift their opinions like the tide. They may also have an explosive temperament that makes it hard for the two of you to see eye to eye on many things.

Those Aquarians born between the 31st of January and the 8th of February will keep you on your toes due to their unusual communication style. These individuals may well scare you off if a chatterbox is not your thing.

The Scorpio–Aquarius combination is complex, but if you're looking to connect with an Aquarian born between the 9th and the 19th of February, this group will be an excellent choice because they have the influence of Venus and Libra. This makes them not only intellectual but sensual and emotional as well.

SCORPIO + PISCES
Water + Water = Deluge

Ah, now here is one of those special, magical unions that most of us only dream of. Scorpio and Pisces blends the powerful and emotional energies of two highly sensitive water signs. This combination can produce an overwhelming amount of uninhibited passion and love. As far as combinations between different pairs of Sun signs are concerned, Pisces is probably the one most suited to Scorpio.

When Pisces works its way into your Scorpio psyche, there's very little you can do except fall head over heels in love, and fall hard you will! Pisces understands intuitively your complex personality and knows just how to tap into your body, mind and spirit. Oh, joy!

At times Pisces can seem to be in some other spiritual realm, where they are so self-absorbed, off on their own mission about who knows what, that they can forget the practical reasons of where they are supposed to be and why they are actually on this planet. They can be in a world of their own, and your practical down-to-earth approach is just what they need. Someone has to go up to 'cloud nine' to collect them every now and again.

The intense and sometimes sarcastic storms of a Scorpio can be well managed by the compassionate Piscean. An example at hand is Richard Burton and Elizabeth Taylor, who couldn't live together, but couldn't live without each other, either. If you, Scorpio, are a rather tormented soul seeking love and understanding in your life, then without a doubt, go search for a Pisces. The love and attachment you're looking for will be manifested beautifully between your Sun sign of Scorpio and that of Pisces.

Pisces born between the 20th and the 28th or 29th of February will give you a lot of sensual satisfaction and, because they are a double-Pisces, their compassionate and idealistic personalities will soothe your weary soul.

There is a very karmic connection with those Pisces born between the 1st and the 10th of March.

Cancer and the Moon have a great deal of influence on these people and many lessons, particularly regarding the emotional self, will be brought out by these Pisceans. Over time some deep insights will be revealed to you if you continue in a relationship with them.

When Scorpio connects with Pisces born between the 11th and the 20th of March, extremes in passion can occur. This group has strong Scorpio tendencies and this can be a powerful but also at times tumultuous combination.

2011:
The Year Ahead

Everything has been figured out, except how to live.

— Jean-Paul Sartre

Romance and friendship

This is the time to look forwards, Scorpio, not backwards! It may seem rather tempting to go back in time and relish the good times that you've had, but now you must seek new vistas in love so that your emotions will continue to grow and your wisdom will ripen.

First and foremost, the most positive omen must surely be the presence of Venus in your Sun sign as the year commences. In January this planet of love and sensuality fully influences your zone of relationships and makes you attractive, charming and easily accessible to all and sundry.

Mars and the Sun with Pluto also cast their energetic and favourable influences on your zone of permanent bonds of friendship, indicating your ability to attract people into your life, but also to work hard at improving the current situation in which you may find yourself.

The outer planets throughout 2011 influence you in a subtle but profound way as well. Saturn, for example, continues its way through your zone of secrets, past activities and karmic influences.

The events of the recent or even distant past may still be playing on your subconscious and you must be very careful, especially throughout February and March, not to allow these subtle memories to be superimposed on your current relationships.

Throughout March things should indeed heat up for most Scorpios. This is a time of great pleasure, creativity and lustful pastimes. With Uranus also still making its impact felt in this area, meeting unusual people, some of who are probably a little off-beat, is not out of the question, and they will most definitely entertain you during this phase of your life.

April takes you into a slightly different arena of love, where your work and your relationships may play a tug of war with your heart. Venus certainly brings with it some opportunities to explore new relationships, but the full force of Mercury, Jupiter, the Sun and Uranus, as well as Mars, mean that you may have little time to enjoy the opportunities that present themselves. This will all be a matter of prioritising and making a firm decision on what you feel is important.

Throughout May frustrating influences cause you to feel restless with life. Firstly, the tough opposition aspect between Mars, Venus and Saturn could play havoc with your emotions if you let it. On the other hand, this is once again a prime opportunity for you to experience the joy of meeting your emotional responsibilities head on and accepting them as part of your life's development.

You will need to get real and honestly speak about how you feel, even if this tends to create a backlash from the person with whom you're trying to be honest. It can make it rather difficult to feel comfortable about being honest if others whack you over the head with a sledgehammer every time you do it. You must explain to your spouse or partner that if you're going to be honest (and yes, this may cause some pain), they should at least graciously acknowledge your effort in being forthright with them.

With the entry of Jupiter into your zone of marriage and long-term committed relationships in June, this period, particularly up until August, will be one in which all of your emotional, physical and possibly even spiritual energies are activated and focused on the object of your love. For many Scorpio-born individuals, this is an elevating period in life, and one which, for the first time in twelve years, could even bring marriage or at least a live-in situation to you.

July is particularly notable as Venus and Mars prod your sensual and sexual energies in the right direction. This will be a highly emotional and transformative time and one in which you could fall madly in love. If I say to you that you need to balance some of these energies, I doubt very much whether you're going to listen because this period also portends a really feel-good time.

Throughout August, when Venus and the Sun are in the uppermost part of the heavens, you will feel an incredible surge of energy and self-confidence. Your powers of persuasion are strong, socially speaking, due to the presence of Mercury and the Moon in your zone of friendships this month. You will spend a large amount of time forging new friendships and exploring new mental horizons.

Don't be too overanxious about making friends in September, however, as you may have a false start. Venus transiting its debilitation sign of Virgo means that your high expectations may not exactly reach the heights you first envisaged. Keep your friendships and your more intimate relationships realistic.

An excellent triangular configuration between the Sun, Venus, Pluto and Jupiter indicate a positive use of power, communication and friendship throughout September, and this means you'll be balancing the forces of love to bring you, and those who are important in your life, much more happiness and self-empowerment overall. An excellent triangular configuration between the Sun Venus and Pluto means that you have the power to improve your romantic opportunities even though the above transits are a challenge. This indicates a positive use of power communication to avert social problems throughout September.

Your ruling planet—or one of them, Mars—enters into the pinnacle stage of its transit in late September and pushes through the mid-heaven around October, signalling another dynamic period of personal achievement and self-confidence. Try not to be too irritable or impulsive in the way you deal with your friends during this phase because, although you mean well, some people could take your intentions wrongly.

In this time frame, it's also likely you could meet someone secretly, or someone from your past, who may still have secret feelings for you, could come out of the woodwork and confuse you. As long as you have your values intact you won't stray, for they will keep you on the straight and narrow.

Throughout November, Venus again quickly returns to your Sun sign and this time Mercury and the Sun add their touches of colour to make you poetic, musical or artistic in some way. Mars, which continues to remain in the upper zone of your horoscope, will provide you with continuing zest and self-confidence to try your hand at something new and original. Sport as well could be a focus for you and would be an ideal way for you to decompress some of the tension you may be feeling in your relationships.

You're fortunate to continue having the pleasing influence of Jupiter in your marital zone. If previously, for example, you have been reluctant to take a friendship to the next level, Mars's entry into your zone of life fulfilment generates excellent vibrations with Jupiter which, in turn, could give you that little nudge you need to go the extra distance with someone. In any case, these last couple of months of 2011 are perfectly indicative of relationships that move to a higher level, offering you the chance of greater inner satisfaction in the months and years to come.

Journeys in December will be pleasant due to the excellent placement of Venus in your third zone of travels. However, try not to obsess and become too rigid in your planning and even, for that matter, in the location you've planned as a destination.

Changes may be necessary and the more flexible you are, the less friction you will feel with those who are involved in this process, particularly leading up to Christmas.

Your ideals, your plans and your cherished dreams for love and romance could finally start to take concrete form in the last month of 2011. This is largely due to the excellent trine aspect forming between Saturn and Neptune. This could also help to give more structure to your family and domestic relationships after a period of some confusion. Some older members of the family will also deliver some important pieces of information that can help you crack open a complex relationship problem at this time.

You may be returning to some older problems; or, having broken up with someone in the past, may finally be able to return to a comfortable level of interaction with them. Keeping the peace will be all important during Christmas 2011 and, with that, I leave you a quote from the Beatles' famous song, which says: 'In the end, the love you take is equal to the love you make.' For you, Scorpio, this is what the final phase of 2011 is all about.

Work and money

Saturn continues to influence your finances by curtailing your expenses throughout 2011. You will naturally want to rein in your spending and over the long term this will be a good thing. Many planets occupy the contractual zone of your horoscope, showing that you'll be making some significant changes in how you communicate to others, sign off on detailed proposals, and also how you ultimately earn your money and improve your cash flow.

You'll be full of energy and ready to make some important changes in January, using your new and up-beat attitude. Take some precautions, however, because you may be overly confident and perhaps could miss some vital clues in your discussions. Try to be flexible in the way you voice your opinions.

When the same planets—Mars, the Sun, and then Mercury—activate your zone of real estate throughout February, you'll be interested in dealing with these issues. Housing and other investments associated with fixed assets will be paramount in your mind. With Venus conjoining Jupiter around the 17th, and then the Sun conjoining Jupiter around the 28th, this period will be extremely lucky for you, so don't worry too much. Let the planets do their work of bringing good fortune to you.

You have some wonderful ideas for improving your working relationships and indeed your work-place itself sometime after the 9th of March, but you could also be obstructed and need to be wary of people who are envious of your successes. It's best to keep a low profile during this phase.

After the 17th some unusual or unexpected changes may occur in your life, so you should be prepared and also have a 'Plan B' ready and waiting in case what you had expected doesn't come to pass.

Business and work are extremely hectic throughout the months of April, May and June. You must be careful not to let your work practices get out of control. Discipline will be an important ingredient in finding a balance in your life, as well as achieving the success you so desire.

You may be working long hours at this time and need to factor in some recreational time to put equilibrium in your life.

Although you may find your working relationships a little overbearing at this time, Venus comes to the rescue and offers you an opportunity to find some peace through creative pursuits.

Be on guard throughout June as competitors and, for that matter, people you work with and possibly even family members, try to oppose you. It's quite likely that a battle of wills can ensue. You need to exercise diplomatic approaches with others.

This is a month when taxation and other elements of finance will be uppermost in your mind. You need to delve into the finer detail of how you're managing your finances. Connections with brokers, financiers, tax agents and perhaps even legal representatives are quite likely during this phase.

A new Moon at this time also heralds the commencement of a new approach in the way you deal with shared money. If you're married or happen to be in a business partnership, discussions centring on a fair and equitable arrangement may also be spotlighted.

You will need to travel throughout July and August to complete some aspects of your work. If you're a commission agent, sales person or someone in marketing, this will be a busy time, but what will be unusual about it is that it may take you away from your normal station or workplace. You may or may not be happy with this arrangement, but you certainly won't be bored. Mercury increases profits and brings extra cash into your hand throughout this time frame.

In September, a Sun and Venus combination activates your social connections. You'll be more readily available to network and make important connections that will help your business and financial opportunities.

Bright ideas are backed up by purposeful action throughout October. This is due to the combined influences of the Sun, Neptune and also Mars transiting the most powerful part of your horoscope. Mind you, the Sun, Mercury, Venus and Saturn produce another parallel thread of energy relating to behind the scenes deals, tricky manoeuvres and secretive liaisons or other dealings. You need to be careful at this time because you may also find yourself the subject of a swindle, theft or loss.

Although the retrograde movement of Jupiter in this latter part of the year indicated frustration that your success is not coming to fruition as quickly as you'd like, Jupiter nevertheless has a positive influence on your relationships and is an excellent omen brining good fortune into your business dealings.

Particularly with Mercury and Venus lending a hand, the last part of 2011 should bring you additional successes whether you expect them or not. Remember with this a double edged sword all good things come to those who wait. Yes, even you, Scorpio, with a little bit of patience will see 2011 out with a smile on your face and some additional cash and opportunities in your pocket. Good luck!

Karma, luck and meditation

Jupiter is one of the most favourable planets for those of you born under Scorpio and its action this year is swift and certain, but probably not until after June. At this time, it moves into your zone of partnerships, marriage and other significant relationships and also brings popularity among the masses.

This is not to say that you shouldn't expect any other sort of luck; there are additional planets such as Venus, which, from January itself, brings some of the most wonderful opportunities to your relationships and social activities. But Jupiter is the primary bringer of good fortune and, after June, you can look forward to a great new cycle commencing both in your marriage and in your business, if you're that way inclined.

Other good luck periods for you, Scorpio, include February, for money; domestic and family satisfaction in March and April; and in particular, passionate and romantic love affairs throughout June. This is in part due to the influence of Venus, one of the other positive planets of the zodiac.

Past karmic influences are shown by the transits of good planets through your ninth zone of karma. Venus once again transits this area throughout the period of July and then enters your career sector in late July and August. These two months should be a wonderful period for you to enjoy the benefits of your past hard efforts, and good karma should now be enjoyed by you.

In September there's a powerful influence of the Sun and Mercury on your social activities. Making new friends, creating a new network or circle of influence will bring you additional good fortune and, if not immediately, this is sure to have its effect sometime in the near future for you.

SCORPIO

Your Bonus 2010 Three Month Forecast

OCTOBER
2010

Highlights of the month

Negotiations can bog down this month, and the reason could be because you're pushing too hard. Use your intuition, which you have in abundance, to sense if the person is feeling awkward or pushed. At the end of the day, you want everyone to be satisfied with the outcome.

Between the 1st and the 3rd there may be additional responsibilities hanging over your head. It might seem like a good idea to get the difficult stuff out of the way early. But if this involves steamrolling someone, it's best to let it slide and not push your own agenda too heavily.

You have strong physical drives throughout October but may also be somewhat accident prone. Try to look at the long-range ramifications of what you're doing. Slow your pace and try not to clock-watch too much. Relish the moment and get into what you're doing to try to produce something of quality rather than of quantity. The key words for you are 'creative satisfaction', especially up until the 7th.

A sudden need to communicate your feelings to someone may take you off course, which in turn will distract you this month. It's important to put your feelings into words so that there's no ambiguity about what you mean.

If, for example, you're planning to take a break from a relationship or, in the extreme, want to break it off completely, it's not a bad idea to articulate how you feel and the reasons for your decision. You have to admit that if things are spelled out plainly, verbally, no one can come back to you with any misunderstandings. It's there in black and white, and you can always refer back to the truth of your statements.

The health of an older member of the family may come into question, particularly after the 8th. Hospitals, asylums and other places not all that pleasant but mainly of a medical nature will draw your attention. Some of you may choose to do some compassionate work that has nothing to do with your responsibilities to relatives or friends who may be unwell or needing help. It could just be that you feel as if you owe your community some service, and this would be a good time for it.

Otherwise, this period could be a professional low because the Sun, your most important career planet, shuffles its way through the quiet zone of your horoscope. Don't try to push things, even if they're going too slowly for your liking. Patience, and nurturing your projects to completion will be necessary.

After the 28th there are indications of a revamping of your pay structure or some legal issues that need full attention. However, with the Sun and Venus empowering you after the 29th, you'll still have a touch of that persuasive charm that will help you get what you want with a positive financial outcome.

Romance and friendship

You may feel ignored or out of the loop between the 1st and the 3rd. Your friends will limit you and you'll feel separated from them and your family. But this sense of isolation and loneliness is not a bad thing. It's of short duration and will help you gain a deeper understanding of life. Serious reflection and introspection proves worthwhile.

Friendships abound between the 5th and the 7th; but there are some clandestine indications mixed in here. Morals will be an important aspect of your lessons and challenges during this phase of the year.

It's quite likely you'll be feeling off the wall and in the mood for entertainment on the 11th and the 16th. Unusual happenings will land you some unexpected surprises. Exceptional solutions will pop up in your head, but you must trust what you feel. Remember that this is a short high: any spurts of positive insight mustn't be lost. Write down your ideas as soon as they come to mind.

Your personality may be at odds with others after the 18th. Accept the fact that there are differences in your personality and you can't force your opinions on others. Not everyone is going to see eye to eye with you. Doesn't matter! Don't lose it over conflicting opinions. You could be challenged, so expect a lot of lead (as in shots) heading your way around this time. Act cautiously to avoid accidents and anger.

Your wellbeing and creativity is peaking between the 19th and the 25th. You'll easily find something fun to do that won't unsettle others. However, this means you could be ready to take a walk because you'll be fed up with the daily grind and a rebellious streak emerges within you.

You'll be able to keep your cool between the 28th and the 30th because you have additional emotional control. Even if someone tries to push your buttons, you won't feel baited.

Work and money

You'll be driven to do your best between the 2nd and the 10th and will want to achieve a great deal. Mars stimulates your professional activities and achievements. This indicates that much of your focus will be on making sure you don't leave anything to chance and will fully realise the benefits of your hard work.

Don't spend too much time daydreaming between the 16th and the 22nd because this can cause you to invest way too much time on ideas that may not be practical. However, planning for the future—as long as it is within the bounds of possibilities—is a good idea.

After the 23rd, you may be instrumental in decompressing a volatile situation between two workmates. By keeping your cool you help promote peace all around you.

Your imagination will be extraordinarily powerful between the 27th and the 30th. Trust your intuition as well because some of the feelings you'll have about others will be quite strong. Your vision for a better future is positive now and should reap some wonderful rewards for you.

Destiny dates

Positive: 4, 5, 6, 7, 9, 10, 23, 24, 25, 27

Negative: 1, 17, 18

Mixed: 2, 3, 8, 11, 12, 13, 14, 15, 16, 19, 20, 21, 22, 28, 29, 30

Highlights of the month

Avoid financial arguments at all costs this month. There's got to be a better way, Scorpio. Mars moving through your zone of finances, income and material values can be problematic, but only if you get too emotionally involved and reactive about other people's opinions. Between the 1st and the 7th, you'll need to set aside ample time to assess your position carefully and that of someone else with whom you either live or work closely.

Sharing the bills, allocating a fair expenditure on different items, will all be up for discussion. Naturally, people have different opinions about these things, but you mustn't let your anger get the better of you. Calm, fair negotiations are in order and will result in a reasonable deal for all concerned.

Once you've carefully assessed and reassessed these financial requirements, the period of the 9th to the 12th reflects Mercury's influence on you to fill out the appropriate forms and send off the paperwork to the authorities to put these commercial issues to bed. After the 12th, your attention will be back on home affairs, with children also coming to the fore between the 14th and the 16th. Get away from business, from the heavy responsibilities of life, and reconnect with your own inner child at this time.

Jupiter's direct movement on the 19th is a great omen and also reflects some of the financial concerns that you've had finally coming to an end. This is a favourable conclusion to any of those lingering, niggling financial issues that you thought you'd never overcome. You can and will come through this and will now be ready to enjoy other aspects of your life more fully.

Between the 22nd and the 29th, there's a good opportunity for you to approach your employer or anyone else in authority from whom you need a favour. Is it an extra amount of money in your pay packet that you're dreaming of? Do you want some more responsibility in your home? Are you looking to extend your home or beautify your living environment? You don't have enough money? Approach the bank manager during this phase. Indications are that the planets will bless you with a favourable response to any requests for help, money or even inner spiritual direction. 'Ask and ye shall receive.'

After the 30th, for some lucky Scorpios, a new relationship could commence that will sweep you off your feet! At this time it's important for you to be aware that even the sort of individuals to whom you'd normally not be attracted are possible soul-mates in disguise.

Romance and friendship

Between the 2nd and the 8th you'll be able to take charge of a romantic situation, even if at times you may be a little shy in coming forward. What are you waiting for? You can stimulate, inspire and redirect your most important relationship in the right direction. Throw your hat into the ring and allow yourself the opportunity to test your mettle.

Your mind moves into an unusual phase after the 9th. You'll be acting rather erratically, wanting something different and out of the ordinary. Although the people you meet now will be exciting and certainly different to your normal peer group, there may not be that much stability on offer.

If between the 14th and the 18th the people or the circumstances in which you find yourself are somehow obstructing what you want to do, you could be using this as an excuse not to get on with it. Believe it or not, some people are afraid of success. You need to be brutally honest in your self-assessment to see whether or not you're sabotaging your own success and projecting this onto others.

You have to bring up some unresolved issues between the 24th and 27th, which may result in you having to deal with such negative human emotions as guilt, shame, jealousy and possessiveness. If you're in a relationship with someone who hasn't yet quite tied up all the loose ends of their past, this could be a large part of the problem that you're dealing with.

You may have overlooked the possibilities in some friendship and only realise the deeper connection with that person around the 28th. This is a time for communicating your feelings if you genuinely perceive a romantic opportunity.

Work and money

Between the 3rd and 7th the budget you have carefully put together or the plan you've been implementing for some time could go completely out the window. Who cares if you binge on chocolate cake, strawberries and champagne for just one night? If you're going to do that, however, don't carry the guilt around with you afterwards.

On the 11th, use your self-control to get through those tasks you've so far been sweeping under the rug. You know that if you keep doing this, you're only going to create an immense amount of work for yourself at some later date.

Some members of your family are not pulling their weight between the 15th and 17th, which could be part of your abovementioned problem. Take control and arrange a work routine for everyone to contribute equally.

It's important to develop a solid emotional basis for your work, especially if you're in a high-stress arena. You'll gain the real benefits of your career around the 22nd only if you've developed your inner poise sufficiently.

Watch your expenses again after the 29th; you're likely to be frivolous and, in the excitement of the moment, may spend more than you can afford.

Destiny dates

Positive: 8, 19, 22, 23, 28, 30

Negative: 17, 18

Mixed: 1, 2, 3, 4, 5, 6, 7, 9, 10, 11, 12, 14, 15, 16, 24, 25, 26, 27, 29

Highlights of the month

The final month of the year could leave you feeling a little weary and worse for wear, but the Sun and Mars empower you so keep a positive attitude around you, at least up until the 20th, when Christmas festivities commence.

You still have loads of charm and Venus's energy to give you successful and fulfilling romantic social episodes. As long as you don't push yourself too hard, do get enough sleep and maintain a good diet, you should be okay. Otherwise, you may find yourself falling asleep for Christmas dinner!

When Mars conjoins Pluto, your two ruling planets, you will feel completely in sync with your own inner power. You may even make a very firm decision to leave a long-term situation. You mayn't act on this immediately, but your mind will be made up. It appears that 2011 may be a brand new chapter in your life!

Travel is very much indicated by these two

planets, Mars and Pluto, transiting your third zone of journeys. If you don't have the opportunity, or your timetable doesn't have enough room for you to take an interstate or overseas journey, you will still be extremely busy running around here, there and everywhere. You may actually bite off more than you can chew, so be careful not to say 'yes' to too many people, particularly if it involves running errands on their behalf.

Parents of children who were born under Scorpio will also be especially busy around the lunar eclipse of the 21st. Educational matters, additional expenses and other unforseen activities will drag you away from a plan you have set for yourself. My recommendation is that you factor in a little extra time for these unexpected demands of youngsters leading up to Christmas.

By far the strongest planets indicating a success-ful and fulfilling conclusion to 2010 will be Venus and Jupiter. These planets continue to offer you luck, especially in your personal life. So I say, 'make hay while the sun shines', Scorpio!

Any uncertainties in any department of your life that have been plaguing you should be clarified and cleared up by the 30th, when Mercury, the planet of thinking, communication and insight, goes forward in direction. The final important transit of the year is the movement of Venus near the position of your Sun in Scorpio. All this adds up to a beautiful end to 2010.

Romance and friendship

You will feel confused between the 3rd and 8th. You may have had dreams of being in a different place by this stage in your life and could become disillusioned if the returns on your input are not quite what you expected. You have to keep the faith and realise there will be highs and lows from time to time. This could be the moment when you take stock of your personal situation.

After the 10th you may have to take a gamble on speaking your mind with a friend. This could be rather difficult, but there's no use beating around the bush. Speak your mind, and if what you have to say doesn't sit comfortably with them, well, that's their responsibility. Don't expect the perfect reaction.

Between the 15th and 24th, if there are some areas of your life that you haven't developed sufficiently, you'll be forced to deal with them in spite of yourself. If you're honest enough about all this, you'll find that it will work to your advantage. You'll feel much better about your association with others and possibly, if a new relationship is offered to you, you'll clearly understand what is necessary for success.

Try to curb your mental restlessness after the 25th. You'll be impatient and won't want to wait for others. If you want their support, try to give them the same level of support you demand back.

Between the 29th and 31st, you could be shocked to find that some of the company you thought was aboveboard and ethical is anything but. It will be important for you to assess coolly the personalities and motives of the people whom you meet. If you're relying on the credibility of someone simply because they're introduced to you by another person who is themselves credible, you may be making a mistake. Watch carefully.

Work and money

After the 14th you have full permission to enjoy a few extra glasses of champagne to knock the edge off your tension, with it being Christmas and all!

What you think of the outside world will now become a reality between the 21st and the 26th. You'll be surprised at how quickly the laws of the universe will make themselves felt. In other words, if you think good thoughts, good thoughts are likely to happen, and so on. Take full responsibility for your thoughts and you'll see very clearly that life throws back at you what you are producing through your own thinking processes.

After the 27th, more investigation on your part may be necessary if you're contemplating a big-ticket item. Don't cut corners by buying cheaply, even if you don't feel that you can afford it. Buy quality in the first place, and you'll be assured of less problems in the future.

As the year comes to a close, channel some of your energy into creative work. You can express your deeper self by the 29th and make some contribution to other people's happiness as well.

Destiny dates

Positive: 3, 4, 5, 6, 7, 8, 10, 14, 26

Negative: 30, 31

Mixed: 15, 16, 17, 18, 19, 20, 21, 22, 23, 24, 25, 27, 29

SCORPIO

2011:
Month By Month
Predictions

JANUARY 2011

I have a simple philosophy. Fill what's empty. Empty what's full. Scratch where it itches.

— Alice Roosevelt Longworth

Highlights of the month

The challenges of January are sufficiently well balanced by the excellent placement of Venus and Jupiter in your horoscope. In the early part of the month you feel somewhat relaxed and confident in your relationships and your creative zest for life should now be peaking.

You'll feel content with your life and at ease with friends and family members up until the 16th when Mars, your ruling planet, but also itself a somewhat impatient and irascible energy, moves into your zone of domestic happiness and family affairs. It's at this time you may run headlong into some problems with close family members. You need to be on guard so you don't react without thought. Words could be spoken that you may later regret.

You have strong ideals for your family affairs, and this is due in part to the presence of Neptune in your zone of properties and family interactions. But you may also be looking at things through rose-coloured glasses. For sometime Saturn has continued to influence your zone of secrets, where your past may still be subtly impacting upon your psychological reactions. So this is a time to be super-aware of your own strengths and weaknesses and accommodate others if you are to improve your life.

The fact that the month commences with a new Moon in this same zone of family affairs highlights the fact that you're ready for change, perhaps even wanting to run to the hills and get away from your current circumstances. This may not be possible at the outset but, by the full Moon of the 19th, you may have some opportunities as well as the desire to travel somewhere; expand your mental and spiritual horizons and do something completely different. A long journey may be in order to help you make sense of where you are on your life's path.

Educational pursuits will stir your curiosity and this is also shown by the Sun and Pluto transiting your zone of intellectual curiosity. Please, Scorpio, don't be so scattered that you end up not doing anything worthwhile. Think things through before you commit yourself to courses of study and research.

On the 23rd, an extraordinary transition of Jupiter into your zone of work, health and daily routine ensures that you will be making some very radical changes in these areas of your life. Jupiter's action, of course, is to expand but also at times to exaggerate.

Due to these above planetary influences, think carefully through such things as your diet, the hours you work and also the company you keep. All these things do compound over time and influence you positively or negatively, depending on how you choose to live your life.

Romance and friendship

On the 1st, 2nd and 3rd of January you needn't let boredom get you down. An entertaining journey to a fabulous rendezvous with someone exciting is quite likely. However, an annoying obstacle in your travel plans may pop up and monetary issues could be at the heart of it.

Travelling to a distant place will be necessary on these dates and will give you perspective as well as help you re-evaluate your life. Don't rush, however. Leave yourself enough time so that your plans flow seamlessly.

On the 4th, your desire to exert your will over a family member will be met with conflict, but between the 5th and 6th use your persuasive powers to win over the heart and mind of someone who is initially difficult to deal with.

Between the 7th and the 10th you'll be oscillating between open love and a cool response to someone who means a lot to you. However, things may pan out much better around the 13th, when you finally discover their true intentions. It's important to find the right balance.

From the 16th till the 19th you experience a red-hot passionate love affair because several newcomers are likely to whet your appetite. Social life is exciting at this time. But you can't quite make up your mind due to indecision over the choices in your romantic life. It's best to wait until after the 26th, when you're clearer.

There are more romantic interests highlighted between the 27th and the 29th. Someone rouses your deepest emotional, or possibly lustful, feelings. Fortunately, these feelings will be mutual.

Great communication is on the cards between the 26th and the 31st. You seem to be talking more than normal, or time is moving much more quickly. The influence of the Moon on your third house of travels and your conscious mind indicates your discussions should be quite satisfying.

Work and money

Your mind is expansive and you're planning some big things this year, particularly between the 1st and the 4th of January. You'll somehow want to share these ideas with others and hopefully they will see your vision. On the 4th you may feel a little overworked, so recharge your batteries if you need to and reignite your passion for the job sometime around the 9th, when the Moon enters your Sun sign.

Work could get a little hectic between the 11th and the 16th. You will, however, still be able to make a great impression on others because you'll be extremely self-confident in the way you put forward your ideas. There's also a good chance you'll find yourself in just the right place at the right time. This is excellent as a luck factor for you professionally.

You have tremendous drive and energy between the 17th and the 20th and, when the Moon enters your zone of career around this time, expect some new windows of opportunity to open. I suggest you seize the moment promptly and don't procrastinate.

Don't allow heavy responsibilities to make you feel down and out between the 24th and the 30th. Some of the work that has filled your in-tray may seem a little daunting at first, but you'll get through it.

Destiny dates

Positive: 5, 6, 9, 13, 17, 18, 19, 20, 22, 31
Negative: 11, 12, 13, 14, 24, 25
Mixed: 1, 2, 3, 4, 7, 8, 10, 16, 26, 27, 28, 29, 30

Highlights of the month

Your interest in improving your domestic situation continues throughout February, with the new Moon occurring on the 3rd. You'll be busy formulating new plans for property or renovations. Or, if being an interior designer or moving house is not your cup of tea just yet, you'll certainly be entertaining a lot of people and finding your house the hub of much social activity.

Between the 2nd and the 7th your emotional ideals reach a pinnacle and you're quite likely to meet someone who will inspire you to do better in life. You may even fall in love if you're not quite attached at this point in time. You could find your heart missing a few beats and your head in the clouds. Try to keep it real.

Your communication is strong and is reflected in your purposeful and constructive working patterns. You have some great ideas throughout February and can really make things happen. You become a little obsessive between the 10th and the 14th because you want to perfect the work with which you are associated. This may get other people's backs up, but between the 14th and the 17th you can effectively communicate the reasons why you are doing this, which will sufficiently decompress your workplace relations to make the latter part of the month not only productive but far more easy-going for you.

The full Moon of the 18th occurs in your zone of profession and self-esteem. At this point you'll feel that it's all systems go, and as well as that, your emotional attachment to work is probably greater than it has been for some time. Enjoy your work, be creative and share the fruits of your labour with the people who've helped you get to where you are. Power issues may dominate your business or perhaps your domestic landscape as well, after the 25th.

The intense aspect of Jupiter and Pluto means you need to deal with some rather large egos when you'd prefer to be just getting on with the job in hand. Towards the end of the month, and in particular after the 25th, your investigative nature—which, as we all know, is one of the key characteristics of the Scorpio personality—allows you to discover some new methodologies, some hidden secrets or other important information that will be valuable to you both professionally and personally.

Divided loyalties may also be a problem for you, so balancing people and their demands on you will also be a key ingredient to finding happiness and harmony this month.

Romance and friendship

You'll be feeling pretty excited about things between the 1st and the 3rd of February, with Uranus causing you to be pretty up-beat and quirky. Your confidence is going to help you create some new relationships during this cycle. In particular, on the 2nd, Venus and Neptune make you very idealistic and you are likely to come across someone who meets those standards you've set for yourself in love and romance.

Between the 4th and the 6th you're highly strung and some of your communications may not go exactly the way you intend them to. There's a real danger that miscommunication can occur and, especially if you're trying to explain yourself to a family member, you may put your foot in it. Think carefully before opening your mouth.

Between the 6th and the 10th your public image will be very important and then, around the 16th, you'll find yourself planning an important event or having to dress a little differently for some sort of engagement to which you've been invited. Taking a fresh look at fashion and what's in your wardrobe will be spotlighted.

You could be the centre of attention between the 21st and the 23rd, especially when Mars enters your zone of relationships and creativity on the 23rd itself. You have more energy to put into your relationships but also want to expand your circle of influence.

You are quite emotional in your communications around the 27th. Be rational when it comes to talking about important matters of the heart. Try keeping things a little low-key, even if you miss out on a particularly pleasant social occasion because you need the time to reflect on things a little more.

Work and money

Try doing things in a more innovative way after the 2nd of February. Applying new technologies to old problems will help you to expand your mind and give you a sense that you're progressing in your work.

Between the 4th and the 6th, spend some time dealing with your self-image, because if you've been self-conscious about some aspect of your personality or your work skills, this is the right time to change things and make a greater impression on others.

There are financial opportunities between the 10th and the 17th, but you need to act quickly and have the correct information before diving in, boots and all. You could also find that these investments will tend to pay off fairly quickly and handsomely.

Take the time to be realistic between the 21st and the 25th. Some of your ideas may have creative merit but they may not be received all that well by your employers. Remember to 'sell the benefit, not just the idea'.

You have strong willpower between the 26th and the 28th and have a chance to work long and hard, even under the burden of some heavy responsibilities. At least this will show what you're capable of doing to those who matter.

Destiny dates

Positive: 1, 2, 3, 4, 5, 7, 8, 9, 11, 12, 13, 14, 15, 17, 26, 28

Negative: Nil

Mixed: 6, 10, 16, 21, 22, 23, 25, 27

Highlights of the month

The new Moon of the 4th highlights your need for love and your ability to start new friendships—even, indeed, new relationships—on a good note, with the prospect of long-term associations benefiting you and the other party.

You can feel communicative, progressive and mutually supported in your relationships both now and throughout the whole period of March, particularly with the full Moon of the 19th occurring in your zone of friendships. This will be an exciting time for you to forge new associations, deepen the existing ties you have with others and also to expand your horizons to broaden your scope of self-understanding.

You have some image issues to be dealt with in the first part of the month, but some sudden and positive twists and turns in your working life around the 12th will see you involved in a whole new ball game that can also signify an enhanced reputation and increased profitability for you.

Be careful of words after the 15th, however. You may deflate a situation by saying just a little too much. Don't allow others to bait you with arguments and other trivial forms of dispute. Keep your eye on the goal posts and don't get distracted by petty little ego games, which are quite likely at this time.

After the 20th, many Scorpios will feel a general easing in the work they're doing, and this doesn't only refer to those who are in professional activities in a corporate sense, but also to those of you who are partners at home, taking great pride and pleasure in executing your duties with your children or other relatives. You can feel a sense of achievement, too. The Sun gloriously shines upon you just now and makes you feel energetic and very, very capable.

You have brilliant flashes of intuition this month due to the excellent combination of Mercury and Uranus. However, don't let yourself become too highly strung because as well as giving you dazzling flashes of intuition and creative brilliance, these two planets can also frazzle your nerves if you're not careful.

Challenging aspects at the end of the month between the 21st and the 28th indicate that you must continue to remain cautious, lest you find yourself working too hard in too many different directions without any purposeful goal in mind.

You could seesaw between joyous abandon and serious responsibility around the 28th. The Venus and Neptune idealism at this time softens the blow of Jupiter, Saturn and Pluto, but perhaps not enough to make you feel clear headed. Jot down your thoughts, get active with your planning, and stick to that plan. You can be very methodical in making decisions. Notate your plans and don't be afraid to take your time.

The period of the 17th to the 21st is telling on your health. Don't burn the candle at both ends. Try to establish your priorities and look carefully at how you're spending your time and your resources.

You may feel as if you have to pursue many different lines of activity to make sure that you don't miss the boat. Covering all bases, however, sometimes means you have to spread yourself too thinly and this could have an adverse reaction on your physical wellbeing. Reconsider your dietary strategies and it may well be time for you to rejoin your local gym and get back into an effective exercise regime.

Romance and friendship

Between the 1st and the 5th of March your communication is powerful and convincing. Electric and off-beat relationships also characterise this period as Venus and Uranus influence your zone of romantic and creative affairs.

You will be opinionated and someone might not like this between the 6th and the 9th, but the presence of Mercury provides you with wonderful opportunities for travel, study and activities with friends. You will continue to exchange ideas and learn much about yourself.

Between the 10th and the 12th you'll be the recipient of a gift voucher or opportunity to improve your health and self-awareness. This will further provide opportunities for you to meet friends.

Deliberate on your decisions between the 15th and the 19th. Don't rush into things and don't follow the crowd just because it seems like a fun thing to do. You might later regret your involvement.

Travel should be considered between the 19th and the 21st. However, you may receive some untoward news and could be needed by one of your friends to help them work through some personal dilemma.

From the 22nd to the 24th you're idealistic in love and want the best for yourself. This is also a good time of the year to begin a new romance. If the opportunity presents itself, don't be shy!

You're oscillating between overconfidence and self-consciousness between the 26th and the 31st. Finding a happy balance and not saying much will solve this particular problem.

Don't make decisions hastily on the 31st. You need to think more carefully before committing to a path of action.

Work and money

Even if money is tight between the 2nd and the 6th of March, you still opt to spend lavishly on your home or some other luxury items. Try to be a little more frugal in your expenditures because it's quite likely you don't necessarily need what it is you're going to buy.

You'll be irritated by some of your work commitments between the 6th and the 10th. On the 11th, don't fret about money issues because there's nothing you can do when they actually should be dealt with by experts.

After the 16th you feel more confident and emotionally buoyant about the work you're doing, with the 18th, 22nd and 23rd being excellent days to push forward your plans and ideas and get a positive response from others.

Contracts are important on the 26th, but you'd probably prefer to be having fun. However, if you cut corners just now, you may run into some sort of contractual red-tape difficulties by the 31st.

Try to curtail your desire to overlook the fine print because it will cost you more in terms of time and effort down the track if you are lax in your attention.

Destiny dates

Positive: 1, 2, 3, 4, 5, 12, 22, 23, 24

Negative: 7, 8, 9, 15, 17

Mixed: 6, 10, 11, 16, 18, 19, 20, 21, 26, 27, 28, 29, 30, 31

Highlights of the month

You are hell-bent on achieving your professional and workplace objectives quickly this month, but it might be a mistake to try to force achieving too much too soon. There are no doubt some lucky opportunities, particularly after the 6th, when the Sun and Jupiter bring you a fortuitous meeting or opportunity that is too good to resist. But perhaps you will resist because Saturn, the cautious planet of the zodiac, causes you to do a double-take on what's on offer.

It is the added influences of the Sun and Uranus that cause you to rush, as do Mars and Pluto, which, after the 11th, give you immense drive but also the possibility of injury or accident through your impulsiveness. These influences continue most notably up until the 18th, when Mars and Saturn also challenge you and stifle your energies, creating some sort of frustration and anger, both with yourself and with others. Chill out, Scorpio. You don't have to achieve everything yesterday.

You can get back on track by the 20th, when the Sun and Neptune offer you an imaginative and possibly mental exit to all of your strife. By the 23rd you'll probably be less inclined to worry yourself over money or work because Venus and Uranus bring you in touch with someone who is completely different to you.

Friendships will rest on innovation, originality and uniqueness. You are interested in forging new ties that are not based on old and outmoded ways of thinking. You'll become very taken by either a new person or some new lifestyle change between the 23rd and the 27th. Someone you meet now influences your thinking or your philosophy and causes you to realise that you've been stuck in the old ways and now it's time to make a big change.

Some of these changes will cause you to retreat and this is also expected because the full Moon of the 18th occurs in your zone of secrets and hidden activities. The additional proximity of Saturn to this full Moon means that many hidden parts of your own personality may be uncovered and dealt with just now. There is a strong psychological tinge to what you may experience and your spiritual ideals may be challenged.

The transformation that I'm speaking about is greatly assisted in a positive way by the Sun and Pluto combination on the 28th. Rather than feeling fearful about change, you will embrace it and see that it is necessary if you are to forge a deep and meaningful life for yourself.

Venus's trek through the creative zone of your horoscope is powerful up until the 22nd, so you should take the time to explore your creative impulses and not miss the opportunity.

Romance and friendship

With Mars on the horizon on the 2nd of April, you're likely to be on the war path. Don't take your attitude into social circumstances, however, because others could rile you up. Fortunately, by the 5th, the planets generally cause you to anchor yourself.

Someone—perhaps a soulmate—could cross your path between the 8th and the 10th. Venus brings good fortune in your love affairs and you're right on target for meeting a special person during this period.

Mercury, the Sun and Jupiter in concert bring you further interesting activities between the 12th and the 15th. Renegotiating your relationships and friendships may also be included in the equation and there's no point feeling short-changed, so pipe up and say something if you need to.

Mars and Saturn threaten your peace of mind between the 16th and the 22nd. Irrespective of how much you want from loved ones, you're not likely to be satisfied by them. You'll be frustrated. This is a classic passive–aggressive stance. Talking about your feelings will be better than bottling them up.

Around the 20th there's a softening influence from Venus, which hints at the possibility of you getting away, taking time out and re-evaluating your position. I strongly recommend you do this and, as a result, you can rebuild a beautiful relationship that will ensure your home or your social circle will function more smoothly.

During the Sun's transit of your zone of marriage after the 20th, this and other long-term partnerships will be taken to a new level. Serving the one you love in a spirit of co-operation is spotlighted, particularly when Venus and Uranus have their say between the 23rd and the 28th. This is a lovely, romantic and also zesty period for your love life.

Work and money

The considerable amount of dynamic energy surrounding you between the 2nd and the 6th of April can cause you to rush through your work, only to find yourself left with nothing to do! Boredom can then set in around the 8th, when Venus aspects your Sun sign. Make sure that you plan enough work to keep you going and sufficiently mentally stimulated.

Negotiate a good deal on the 12th so that your position is cemented in the company you happen to work for. By the 14th you'll be endowed with a cash surplus as a result of your clever tactics.

Don't let gossip undermine your self-confidence between the 16th and the 20th. The malicious rumours that you hear may simply be a way of causing you to falter so that others can take advantage of your good position.

You'll find yourself extremely busy between the 21st and the 28th. Pace yourself and once again make sure that your diary is up to date.

Destiny dates

Positive: 3, 4, 5, 6, 9, 10, 12, 13, 14, 15
Negative: 16, 17, 18, 19
Mixed: 2, 8, 20, 21, 22, 23, 24, 25, 26, 27, 28

Highlights of the month

Relationships feature quite strongly for Scorpios throughout the month of May. The new Moon on the 3rd accentuates your most personal and important associations and, particularly if you're married or in a long-term relationship, this month is going to bring to the fore some changes, which should be welcomed by you. But the question is, will they be welcomed by your partner?

With Mars entering your marriage zone on the 13th, you can expect heated debate, or at least differences of opinion, to occur between you and your significant other. Peaceful discussion based upon mutual understanding is the way through at this time.

You can expect more cordial relations between the 9th and the 16th, when Mercury and Venus deliver a much softer energy to your relationships, which will elicit a far better response from those who might otherwise be stubborn and far too opinionated. You can expect, in particular, the Mars and Neptune combination of the 12th to bring some dream to reality.

Around the same time, Venus and Jupiter promise some gift, accolade or feeling of achievement. These two planets are historically noted by astrologers as bringing good fortune and generally a feeling of goodwill between people.

Generally, a large cluster of planets in one area of the zodiac is a telltale sign of an overemphasis of activity, or at least thought, in a particular department of life. For you this month, May, the chart is weighted towards heavy work deadlines, intense responsibilities and possibly far too many irons in the fire. You'll need to make some serious choices concerning your priorities.

By the 20th, Mars, Pluto, Mercury and Venus enter into strong relationships. Pluto and Venus will be with Mars up until the 23rd. Your indomitable energy will achieve a great deal and this is also a time for you to test your willpower as well as your limits. You'll feel as if there's nothing you can't do.

You will have a broad mind, far-reaching goals and the energy and drive to achieve your objectives. You also have the support of the people you work with and those you love. However, with Venus moving into the opposition of Saturn, you can probably feel that some of the support you receive from your nearest and dearest is more or less a token gesture and not coming completely from the heart.

After the 24th you feel particularly amorous and lucky in your relationships as well as your social activities. You can thank Venus and the Sun for such good fortune. Romantic affiliations are very strong and you are likely to experience an increase in passion around the 25th, 26th, 30th and also the 31st.

Romance and friendship

Your passion for love is obstructed between the 1st and the 5th of May. Venus and Saturn don't allow you to share your deepest and most intimate secrets easily with your lover. In fact, secrets will be part of your dilemma just now as you try to balance honesty and transparency with self-protection.

Humour and genuine expressions of love are likely from the 12th until the 14th. On the 16th, there's a strong possibility of recommitting to someone, or at least getting clarification from them on their feelings. You are creative around the 17th and can take on a course or activity.

You don't necessarily have to get on with neighbours. This will be clear after the 20th when you'll clash with them over trifling matters. Get things in perspective because it's pointless creating a feud over something so trivial as a fence or the look of a plant.

When the Sun transits into your zone of deep sexuality and shared feelings, you will push your relationship in a direction that the other party will not feel comfortable with. On the 21st and 22nd, be sensitive to their needs. If you can do so, both your passions and those of your partner can be aroused by the 23rd, when Venus and Mars enter into a strong, loving configuration.

Dare to be different on the 25th. Get out there, be exciting and use your best talents to win a lover, particularly if you've been single for way too long. It's party time! Up until the 29th you can enjoy dancing, laughing and, most of all, attending functions and other interesting events. You'll have more than one opportunity to engage in romance and other passionate sidelines.

On the 30th, watch your step; both figuratively and literally. Mars could cause you to slip and fall, and with Mercury entering to a hard aspect to the Sun, your words could get you into a spot of bother.

Work and money

You're feeling much more comfortable and confident in your dealings with the public. Get out there and have a go, especially after the 2nd of May, when the Moon makes you more emotionally connected with clients and business partners. Up until the 5th you can hammer at a deal and gain some benefits for yourself and your team.

From the 7th up until the 12th, pay strict attention to any contracts that may be out of date or wording that doesn't enhance your cause, especially if you're a wheeler and dealer. If you happen to be a home-maker or someone not involved in the professional arena, don't let slick salespeople take your money too quickly. Read between the lines and don't trust anyone.

You may lose some money on the 14th, so be careful where you place your valuables. A quick succession of events between the 18th and the 26th ensures a busy period involving money, quick journeys, negotiations over tax and other financial investments. Balance your time and also schedule your work accordingly so that it doesn't impact upon your personal life.

Reduce your workload between the 27th and the 30th because you're likely to be overtired.

Destiny dates

Positive: 13, 21, 22, 23, 24, 25, 26

Negative: 1, 3, 4, 16, 20, 30

Mixed: 2, 5, 7, 8, 9, 10, 11, 12, 14, 27, 28, 29

Highlights of the month

As the middle of the year comes upon you, you will need to make some important decisions involving your personal and shared finances. Venus and Mars continue to activate your zone of partnerships, so this and any other financial actions that require the go-ahead by someone else will be important.

Money and its uses will be a key factor in your activities throughout June and the new Moon on the 1st, which occurs in your zone of shared resources, means you'll have to discuss the ins and outs of these issues with others. You will be clever in figuring out how to improve your financial worth, how to save money and also how to spend it much more wisely. But this requires consultation and quite a bit of give and take if you are to avoid arguments over the almighty dollar.

You can lighten things up considerably with the entry of Venus into your zone of sexual activity around the 10th. Try to involve yourself with your partner's desires and look at it as a creative interaction that will not only make you feel good but will open the doors of imagination.

The full Moon of the 15th will bring you in touch with your own feelings and give you an insight into the higher forces of nature, spirituality and other ethical and moral points of view. These factors are even more pertinent due to the entry of the Sun into your ninth zone of religion, higher education and philosophical viewpoints.

You'll be much more interested in understanding life which, in turn, will give you a sense of exhilaration and exploration. You will be balancing the old with the new. Eliminating many of your outdated views and values of the past will lift you to a whole new level of understanding, broadening your life opportunities. This is certainly the time when you will reach a new level in your life.

Towards the end of the month you will have opportunities to invest money creatively; but don't be too rash around the 26th, when a workmate or someone close to you offers you a tip that may not be based so much on research and good information as on hot gossip coursing through the grapevine.

Siblings may well be a source of concern for you in the last few days of the month. Try not to force the issue which may be troubling one of your brothers or sisters. You are indeed correct in your assessment through your keen observation, but this may not be an appropriate time to talk to them.

Romance and friendship

Far from being afraid of responsibility, the period of the 1st until the 5th of June will cause you to embrace it. You see this as a period of tests, where you want to prove to others you are capable of being reliable and of displaying a level of integrity that is becoming of who you are as a person.

After the 6th, if the relationships you've had have been feeling flat, you will want to expand your understanding of them and gain greater happiness in your love life or marriage. Try to extend your hand in friendship and coax your partner into getting therapy and studying self-help books, or simply getting out and attempting something different with you.

Mercury, in friendly aspect to Uranus around the 7th, brings with it some humour; a taste for the bizarre and different. You'll meet some friends or at least create some sort of spectacle in the home during this interval.

At the same time, excellent aspects from Venus, Jupiter and Mars provide you with exciting and diverse relationships and interactions between the 9th and the 15th.

An important lunar eclipse on the 16th reveals that your feelings may be due for a shake up. It's best not to be too emotional, particularly about the past and, if you happen to meet someone who isn't exactly the nicest of characters, you have to deal with them. Don't let your feelings get the better of you. The 17th till the 20th will be notable for you losing some measure of control.

Around the 21st, a secret affair—either that of a friend or even your own—is highlighted. Trying to resolve issues of guilt and other negative human emotions will be an important component of your growth and self-development.

A battle of wills could ensue around the 28th. Sometimes it's better to concede simply for the sake of peace.

Work and money

There could be a blind spot in your business dealings, especially on the 2nd of June, when a solar eclipse relating to your financial dealings or, in fact, your financial value system, could unleash some uncontrollable energies.

You may realise there are some facets of your business, or the way you deal with money, that have not been disciplined enough. Take full control of your money and, if someone else has been calling the shots, you now need to change the situation.

An excellent business decision between the 5th and the 10th ensures a good, solid foundation for future growth. Take the time now to use your skills and the wisdom you've gained in the past through your job to move into something bigger and better. You mustn't let fear or cold comfort stand in the way of your success.

You must learn to save time. With the excellent power of Mercury you can make effective use of words from the 11th till the 15th via telephone, the Internet and other modern technologies, to reach the maximum number of people with the least effort.

You'll get some good responses through these communications, but there is a danger of being overloaded by shoving too much in one end of the pipe only to find that it starts coming out the other end. You need to delegate and have a few additional measures in place if things get too busy.

The period of the 17th till the 23rd will be possibly exhausting, although successful, for you.

An unexpected call or visit after the 26th could give you an even greater boost to your personal prestige and bank account.

Destiny dates

Positive: 1, 3, 4, 5, 6, 7, 8, 9, 10, 11, 12, 13, 14, 15, 26

Negative: 17, 18, 19, 20, 21, 22, 23, 28

Mixed: 2, 16

Highlights of the month

Travel is a fascinating topic to you this month. But if you're feeling as though there are other pressing problems that aren't allowing you the opportunity to get away, then you'll simply have to relegate this idea to a future 'to do' tray on your desk. Between the 1st and the 4th, try to get hold of travel brochures, talk with others who've been able to get cheap fares, and question those who've travelled the world and have an insight into the best destinations. By planning effectively and by doing this over a long period of time, you can create a great holiday schedule that will be second to none.

Apart from the fact that you may be planning long-distance journeys, the full Moon of the 15th also shows that you'll be extremely busy this month. Mercury, the planet of communication, moves into your career zone and this could herald the beginning of a few weeks of very intense travelling, errands and other numerous telephone and Internet discussions. Your e-mail inbox may be fuller than usual and you could find yourself spending a lot of time trying to get rid of junk mail or catching up with old friends who've been left on the backburner for a while.

You'll need to hone your conversational skills during the month of July, because Mercury will put you in the limelight and your ability to communicate ideas will be scrutinised very deeply by your co-workers and your employers. If you're looking to improve your financial status you'll come to realise that the way you express yourself has a marked impact upon the way others will perceive you and help you as well. For some Scorpios, this is an excellent month to forge ahead in career matters and even possibly apply for new jobs, get some first-rate interviews, or receive a promotion.

You'll want to continue exercising your strong physical drive this month through taking on a new exercise regime, challenging physical activity or outdoor hobby. With Mars also transiting the precarious zone of your horoscope, I advise you to take every precaution necessary to avoid mishaps. This may also be related to your lack of self-care, hygiene or general wellbeing. Sleep more, take your vitamins and don't take on too much work. Of course, make sure you take enough warm clothing with you if the weather is cool because you're likely to catch a cold.

In particular, when Mercury and Neptune challenge each other, this is a time when not only your physical health but your mental and emotional health need to be kept in tip-top condition. This influence may be most notably felt between the 27th and the 31st. Take care of yourself and remember to laugh a little more than usual because this is the perfect antidote to any sort of stress that can undermine your immune system.

Romance and friendship

You will want to stabilise your emotional energies by practising some creative pastimes. On the 1st, 3rd and also the 8th of July, your involvement with a loved one in such things as music, crafts or other artistic pursuits will help improve your relationship and take it to a new level.

You mustn't be led up the garden path between the 10th and 13th, because a friend may have suggestions that negatively affect you mentally or emotionally and also have physical consequences. Stay away from alcohol, drugs or other dubious activities. It's not a time to let temptations steer you off the straight and narrow.

You'll feel responsible for the behaviour a friend between the 15th and the 22nd. By taking on their troubles, your self-sacrifice may certainly bring them an enormous amount of satisfaction but you could also end up having to clean up the mess they are in.

Communications will be difficult between the 24th and the 26th, not because you or your friends openly want to contradict each other, but because significant issues may be overlooked. Get some clarity when you are talking to them and don't assume anything.

Between the 27th and the 29th, Venus provides you the opportunity to engage in several discussions centred around your ethics and spiritual interests. You may find yourself expressing different views to friends. It may be best to say as little as possible.

Due to the combination of Mercury and Neptune, misunderstandings are likely around the 30th. However, these minor differences shouldn't be blown out of proportion and some patience will ultimately bring more stability to your life.

At the same time you mustn't let emotional concerns bother you too much. If you have some guilt or shame regarding the past that is bothering you, it could have an adverse effect on your health. Seek some professional guidance.

Work and money

Be careful that money doesn't become a power play during July as Jupiter, your ruling financial planet, moves into a strong rendezvous with Pluto. You will want to spend much more than you have but will have someone else to contend with who may have other ideas. Try to deal with such things as debts and other unexpected expenses between the 1st and the 8th.

Between the 11th and the 20th periodic payments such as car insurance, home and contents cover, superannuation and other annoying expenses may seem like an avalanche. Just try to plan more carefully for your future financial security. Notwithstanding these challenges to your personal expenses, the period of the 23rd to the 27th indicates new streams of income that add value to your company or business.

A dispute over money should be avoided around the 28th and peaceful negotiations can be entered into. Don't hold grudges if someone is driving a hard bargain. Keep it fair.

Things can turn around on the 30th as long as you don't let your thinking become confused by unclear objectives. Plan more effectively before entering meetings.

Destiny dates

Positive: 23, 27, 28, 29

Negative: 10, 11, 12, 13

Mixed: 1, 2, 3, 4, 5, 6, 7, 8, 15, 16, 17, 18, 20, 21, 22, 24, 25, 26, 30

Highlights of the month

Even if for sometime you've felt as if the circumstances around you are somewhat out of your
control, you needn't worry too much in August
because the Sun and Venus bless you with their
powerful vibrations from the upper part of the
heavens. You will be completely capable of trans-
forming even adverse circumstances into your
favour. The difficult position of Mars also shifts into
the positive upper part of your horoscope after the
4th, so it's 'all systems go' with a positive spin on
most things.

You can feel really great about yourself this
month, and I mean really great, because the full
Moon on the 13th fully activates that part of your
horoscope relating to your emotions. For some
reason you'll feel much more loving to others and in
tune with family members, in particular.

Because the Moon has much to say about your
mother, why not take the time to connect more

deeply with her? Females generally will also have a greater part to play in your life just now. If you need to achieve something, get a favourable decision, move forward in some direction, the assistance of females will greatly aid you in this respect. In short, women will be a great resource for you throughout the month of August.

Romantic surprises are on the cards this month, with Venus and Uranus creating a favourable influence for you. The unexpected is likely to happen within your work arena. Could this possibly be a workplace romance? Perhaps, but that comes with its own downside, as you know. Be careful before jumping out of the pan and into the fire. Be particularly mindful of this scenario around the 27th, when the Moon also joins this planetary combination, making you highly emotional and susceptible to weird and wonderful individuals.

Mars provides you with great fuel for study, education and intellectual curiosity. Its presence in your zone of higher education continues for a month or so, so avail yourself of the educational resources at your disposal to increase your skill set, both for work and personal pleasure. Home sciences, interior design, or nursing, caring or social work seem to be some of the areas that might be highlighted as points of interest for you this month.

Mercury can cause some initial confusion over a friendship; perhaps a misunderstanding due to words not being heard properly or assumptions being made when you should really be getting clarification. Don't let the fog of confusion overburden you or complicate your peer group relationships. If you have any doubts, ask questions, and this will clear the air and give you the chance to deepen your relationship with your closest friends.

Romance and friendship

You're really excited about your romantic prospects during August due to the extraordinary combination of Venus and Uranus. Your lucky stars hint at a romance that can bring happiness, even though the promise of a long-term commitment may not be there.

Enjoy love and friendship between the 1st and the 4th because this could be a memorable time.

Your diet takes centre stage after the 5th and you become increasingly aware that your wellbeing is all about what you eat. Your moods and physical state will benefit from some sort of dietary improvements.

You'll be pleased when friends notice the changes that are starting to take place due to your new resolution to look good! Your self-image also improves, but try harder to make it about your health rather than appearances.

You're very edgy and uncomfortable with the company you keep between the 7th and the 11th. You might find yourself acting impulsively. Ask some serious questions before moving passionately into relationships. 'The devil is in the details', as they say, but you mightn't care less. You should! A letter or text message will clarify matters and you can expect an upliftment of your spirits on the 22nd.

Between the 24th and 26th do favours for others but don't let them take advantage of you. You mustn't let the word get out that you're the local community welfare agency. You will, however, feel satisfied in helping someone with a problem because you have a strong compassionate streak.

Hard work on the home front between the 28th and the 30th will squeeze you for time and you could regret you don't have enough of it for other personal activities.

It's a physically exhausting cycle for you at the moment, with work commitments placing additional strain on your relationships. Sharing the load with your partner will create more passion between you.

Work and money

Between the 3rd and the 5th of August, contracts are on the cards when a friend brings you in touch with some mutual commercial interests. A favour will be returned to you due to good karma. A new undertaking with someone more mature should be considered worthwhile after the 8th.

From the 14th until the 18th, investments will be beneficial. You'll be fortunate and should have access to a friend who is well studied in such things as the stock market or other forms of financial management.

Around the 20th an acquaintance could try to 'swindle' you of your hard-earned cash, even though it may be a harmless attempt on their part to help you make money. Be careful. Watch unnecessary flattery.

Meanwhile, the 21st to the 26th indicates that someone is trying to get hold of your trade secrets or information about how you do business. Be careful of their intentions—they're not aboveboard.

By the 30th you will boost the value of your home and also save money surrounding these matters. Altering the method of your payments on your home loan will help reduce the interest bill.

Destiny dates

Positive: 1, 2, 3, 4, 5, 14, 15, 16, 17, 18
Negative: 7, 9, 10, 11, 20, 21, 23, 28, 29
Mixed: 8, 22, 24, 25, 26, 30

SEPTEMBER
2011

Highlights of the month

The conjunction of the Moon and Saturn in your zone of secrets and personal suffering is highlighted when the full Moon of the 12th takes place in your zone of romance.

There may be some issues lingering from a past relationship that you haven't been able to let go of. Friends can assist you in this matter, but it's quite likely, from what I see in your horoscope, that you'll want to grin and bear this alone. Friends may want to help but can actually end up being a distraction in getting to the bottom of your problem and releasing yourself from your past. These are important issues that you should address throughout the first couple of weeks of the month.

Neptune, the idealistic and spiritual planet, hovers just on the cusp of your zone of family and zone of romance and love affairs. Until you clear up your past issues, you may be ill-advised to rush off into another relationship, even though Venus and the Sun are prodding you from your zone of friendships and social interactions. You must be realistic to achieve the emotional satisfaction you so desire.

You mustn't be surprised if a friend in need puts the hard word on you this month. Venus, which is the planet of compassion for Scorpio-born natives, transits through your zone of friendships. Being in the sign of Virgo, which represents service, assistance and love for love's sake, you may find yourself reaching out to someone in need to help them.

Be careful in the second part of the month when these transits are more likely to be a problem for you, particularly between the 19th and the 23rd. In fact, you may end up kicking yourself by the 24th when you realise that you may have been a little too impulsive in extending your hand in friendship and help. Matters could be even more complicated if the requirement involved money.

One positive benefit of Venus in your zone of friendships is that this particular part of your horoscope also represents profitability. This is excellent news, especially if you work for a commission or are involved in any sort of business partnership, because this planet promises to bring you some extra cash that will, no doubt, be welcomed.

The new Moon on the 27th also occurring in this sector promises some new sources of income or a discovery that will surprise you. You may start to take an interest in creating a home business or could pool your resources with a friend to start earning a little bit of cash on the side.

Romance and friendship

Between the 1st and the 5th of September, friends may not appreciate your creative attitude.

Meaningful relationships must be balanced against your own personal desires between the 9th and the 13th. There will also be some strange challenges arising from people in your immediate social circle. Perhaps they're testing your loyalty to see if you are genuine. You mustn't react too strongly; just play along with it.

After the 15th, when Mercury and Jupiter form a favourable aspect to your marriage zone, your basic motivation to work hard on your relationships is focused. Sorting out any problems in relationships that previously have been bogged down should now be easy.

Others will appreciate your attention in helping them between the 17th and the 23rd; however, be careful to choose the right time and place if you extend your hand in generosity. You'll feel somewhat obliged to help someone who doesn't really deserve it but you don't want to appear mean-spirited.

Around the 25th Mercury provides you with the mental energy and opportunities to enhance your romantic circumstances. You will take full advantage of any chance meetings with others. A new love affair can take off. Taking time to improve your communication skills will be met with delightful responses.

The planetary forces between the 26th and the 30th require your wholehearted attention to the person you love if you want to develop a successful and trusting bond. During these last few days of the month, you could be so committed to making sure everything is 'right' with them that you'll temporarily alienate yourself from other friends. But it will be necessary to prioritise people in your life.

Work and money

Work-related journeys between the 1st and the 9th of September are anything but tedious, so allow yourself extra time to get to your destination and mix your career with some pleasure. Delays or misunderstandings about the purpose of your travel may surface around the 8th. You need more transparency in your expression.

Financial matters will be uppermost in your mind between the 10th and the 15th. Have you gone overboard and spent more than you've actually earned? It's quite likely you're paying a higher price than expected for something based upon your impulses. Reject poor advice and trust your instincts.

Don't take your working life for granted. Between the 17th and the 25th, appreciate the ups as well as the downs. Sometimes it's too easy to expect the grass to be greener on the other side. Some of your professional decisions will be rather casual, so take the time not only to appreciate your current situation but to let others know you appreciate them as well.

After the 27th, nervous tension within you may result in errors of judgement. Stop, look and listen!

Destiny dates

Positive: 6, 7, 26, 28, 29, 30

Negative: 14, 15

Mixed: 1, 2, 3, 4, 5, 8, 9, 10, 11, 12, 13, 17, 18, 19, 20, 21, 22, 23, 24, 25, 27

Highlights of the month

Work this month may be conducted in a more private manner. Your best successes will occur by isolating yourself and working away from prying eyes. When the Sun enters your zone of friendship, it is always an extraordinarily good time for socially extending your hand to others.

From the latter part of September through till the 23rd of October, you can expect some new and exciting relationships to start really inspiring you. Over the next month or two, friendships are going to be a very definite and defining factor in your life.

You'll also want to link yourself with those who are strong, successful and, in terms of their character, very powerful. You're looking for a way to increase your self-worth and become more readily recognised by others. Because of this you'll find yourself participating in group activities and community based services that will link you to others who exhibit these qualities you are now looking for.

Your thinking becomes progressive this month, which also involves meeting new and smart people. Mercury, too, is a planet that relates to humour, so you can expect to share a few good laughs with those you hang out with. Communication, working on clever dialogue and also studying more about sociology or life in general will be a common point of interest for you and your friends.

You'll also now have an opportunity to plan or accomplish something novel by getting more involved with your friendships, both existing and new.

Venus moves through your zone of secrets this month, but in this position, Venus makes you quite luxurious in your tastes and your expenditure may also be quite high. You may need to be a little more cautious about the way you spend your money and remember that you can still purchase things that look great without bankrupting yourself.

Your desire to plan and formulate a new direction in your life, especially in your career arena, is accentuated by the movement of Mars in the upper part of your horoscope. You're highly motivated during October and your perseverance will ultimately lead you to some great successes.

You won't be afraid to take on more responsibility and your self-reliance and abilities all round will make you more in demand. In particular, from the 13th to the 20th, these influences will be most strongly felt. But just a word of caution: if you have someone who recently has become a problematic personality, it could be a good idea to distance yourself from them.

Romance and friendship

From the 3rd until the 13th of October you need to work through your feelings of inadequacy and not project negative feelings onto others. Also, someone close will exhibit jealousy and let you know it in not too many words. You'll have to rise above pettiness.

It will be hard to maintain positive feelings between the 14th and the 18th, but look at the bright side. It's best to stay away from those who have a tendency to be glum about things. This applies more specifically to family members who are trying to cut down tall poppies.

Someone from your past may re-emerge and bring back many of those loving and/or mixed emotions you have about them. Between the 19th and 22nd you will have to put up a protective barrier to stop these feelings from drowning you. Be cordial, but don't give away too much.

Expect a rather enjoyable message or letter after the 23rd. This may stir you to improve yourself because it will inspire you. A visitor might arrive around the 27th and this will give you the opportunity to share some recent experiences.

The new Moon on the 26th is in the area of your self-undoing. You may be living life too hard and fast for your own good. Slow the pace and take care of your health—both mental and physical.

You will be the recipient of a gift after the 29th, but don't expect this to solve all your problems because it may simply be a token to alleviate someone else's guilt for doing something wrong.

Work and money

Expenses will spin out of control between the 2nd and the 10th of October, but you can get back on your feet financially if you try. Your earning capacity ranks highly due to the fabulous position of Jupiter and its influence on you. You will attract some new opportunities to increase your income.

Money is a hot topic for you on the 14th and the 17th, and you'll probably be wondering why you never saw such creative financial possibilities before. Your excitement about money and its uses will be connected to those who can instruct you in developing your skills in this area.

Some business partner or co-worker causes you to feel hemmed in between the 22nd and the 26th. This requires you to call an important meeting to share your feelings and ask them to accommodate your skills. There may be a sense that you're being short-changed, either financially or in terms of credit, for the work you're doing.

After the 27th and up to and including the 29th you will feel extremely constructive in the way you are doing your work. Try not to let a momentary lapse in judgement on the 30th cause you to be overly extravagant.

Destiny dates

Positive: 27, 28, 29

Negative: 11, 12, 13, 24, 25, 26, 30

Mixed: 2, 3, 4, 5, 6, 7, 8, 9, 10, 14, 15, 16, 17, 18, 19, 20, 21, 22, 23

Highlights of the month

You can make a few quick but significant changes throughout November and, leading up to the 7th, this may have to do with your environment and also dietary and medical factors. You may find that some sort of medical advice you have received is not working and you could be rather confused about the conflicting advice you're getting through friends and family.

It's a period when you need to research, to go beyond your normal scope of understanding, to get to the bottom of the problem. Your health issues might not be all that serious, but if you're not treating them correctly, the spin off could be that the medication, herbs or even the diet you're taking is exacerbating that particular problem. Use your intuition as well. Between the 1st and the 10th, step outside your normal way of doing things to consult with some alternative practitioners, for example, who may give you clearer insights into your health and wellbeing.

When Mars trines Jupiter around the 16th, you have some extraordinary ideas as well as energy to overcome lethargy or apathy. At this time you'll want to do something extravagant and perhaps even dramatic. Why not throw a party and invite all your friends? What's the occasion? Who cares? Have some fun and enjoy the beneficial energies of these two planets, which are very favourable for those born under Scorpio.

Mars, in its transit through your zone of friendships, continues to accentuate your need to be with others. But, by the same token, there are other sides to this story that could include getting too close and too familiar with someone who could start to irritate you. Using some give and take and sometimes making yourself scarce are probably better ways of improving rather than damaging your friendships at this time.

An important new Moon takes place on the 25th in your Sun sign, indicating a brand new cycle, reflecting a brand new you! Venus and Mercury, as well as the Sun and then the Moon, all promise to lift your spirits at this later stage of 2011. It's as if you're re-creating yourself now and, with Jupiter's continuing lucky influence in your zone of relationships, it's likely you'll start to feel much more satisfaction within yourself.

Dare to be different at this time, even if you get some sideways glances from those who normally give you unflinching support. You don't need to do everything like everyone else and this is the time when you can step outside of the norm and explore life in a thoroughly different manner.

After the 22nd you can expect your long-term relationships to enter into a more stable phase. You're clearer about what you want and, in turn, your partner, spouse or lover may also sense that and feel more comfortable in telling you how they feel. Around the 27th, be careful that your erratic behaviour doesn't get friends offside.

This is indeed a lucky month for you and will prove to be one of the most important ones in the year for your self-esteem and forging new bonds of love with others.

Romance and friendship

You'll have rich emotional experiences up until the 10th of November. The full Moon affects your relationships in such a way as to make you feel much more appreciated by the one you love, and this in turn will feed the relationship more positively. Journey with your lover for a weekend away. It will be emotionally rewarding for you.

There is a very energetic tone to your relationships between the 11th and the 15th. You are actively seeking new friendships and will go out of your way to find people who meet your criteria. This could be precipitated by someone causing you some angst. If you have a friend who has been insensitive and making excessive demands on you, it may be time to step away from them.

Between the 16th and the 20th there could be news you hear on the grapevine that is a little confusing. Receiving mixed messages causes you to doubt a friendship. Wait a couple of days before saying anything because you are most probably projecting your insecurities onto them.

The new Moon of the 25th indicates that you may have to make time to improve your physical condition. Eliminate any health concerns you are worried about. Get a check-up, even if you don't particularly like going to the doctor, because this will give you peace of mind.

You could find yourself on the Internet and taking a greater interest in online dating around the 30th. This will benefit you. Watch how people interact and learn about this form of communicating to further your romantic possi- bilities. Venus makes you more attractive and desirable during this phase as well.

Work and money

Educational matters interest you, and a good time to combine them with your professional activities will arise between the 1st and the 4th of November. Ask your boss to cover the costs of any related studies that come to light, even a correspondence course. This will expand your mind and give you a sense that you're gaining more out of your profes- sional life.

You feel lethargic between the 7th and the 12th. You can't get much done and, the more you force yourself to do, the less inclined you will be to achieve. It's best to take a few hours or even a day off to recharge your batteries and start afresh.

Stress, which is on the increase in your professional relationships, needs to be decompressed during the period of the 15th to the 23rd. Express yourself physically and get into doing more sports; otherwise, you are likely to become so irritable that you'll even get your best friends offside.

Why not consider taking a greater interest in your hobbies after the 24th, because this will be a time when work is the last thing on your mind. You need to find the happy medium between business and pleasure.

Destiny dates

Positive: 1, 2, 3, 4, 5, 6, 13, 14, 24, 30

Negative: None

Mixed: 7, 8, 9, 10, 11, 12, 15, 16, 17, 18, 19, 20, 21, 22, 23, 25

Highlights of the month

In looking at your horoscope for the last month of 2011, I can't help but give you a preview of the great responsibilities that lie ahead. I say this to you because of the impending movement of Saturn through your Sun sign over the course of 2012.

You may not know why, but you'll start to feel, once again, a deep need for change and a restructuring of your life. The fortunate thing is that Jupiter will continue to influence you with its positive vibrations, and therefore the changes that you sense won't be too overwhelming. This again has much to do with your relationships and the courage you will need to make the changes that are necessary. This is all a matter of honesty with yourself and others.

Between the 1st and the 10th, the full Moon occurring in your zone of shared resources is a telling sign on the fullness you feel emotionally about your work and life purpose.

The Moon is a lucky planet for you. But here you will sense that, although this luck has to do with your shared resources and money, much of its influence will also relate to your career. The Sun and the Moon, both being involved this time, will affect your professional activities.

There will be ample evidence of new sources of income, with others being more likely to advance finance to you and be generous with gifts and other sorts of introductions and life opportunities. It is Christmas, after all. So, Scorpio, you can probably expect a bigger-than-usual gift from someone this year!

Once again, the new Moon that occurs around the 24th will highlight your earning capacity. These influences will be felt very strongly leading up to this date, from probably the 15th onwards. Work hard, think clearly and by all means be a team player at this time. Don't, however, obsess about contracts or where you feel you've been short-changed because Venus and Pluto, along with the favourable aspect of Mars, indicate that you'll get what you want but you shouldn't push too hard for it.

At the end of the day, 2011 should be a successful year for you, offering you many new insights into your personal and professional activities. The added bonus you will have comes from the influence of some spiritual energies that lift your self-awareness to bring you greater peace of mind.

Take advantage, in particular, of the opportunity to get away and enjoy the company of friends from afar. The final few days of the month indicate your desire to travel and enjoy. But if you can't physically travel, then make the effort to contact people with whom you haven't been in touch for a while. You'll gain a great deal of pleasure from such communication as the year comes to a close.

Romance and friendship

Obsession characterises your love life through-out the period of the 2nd to the 6th of December. However, there's no need to feel like this, because the harder you try, the less you will achieve. Relax a little and let life do the work for you. If someone is interested in you, they will show their feelings to you soon enough.

A brand new romantic opportunity will spice up your life between the 7th and the 10th. You have to open your heart to new possibilities, even if you think you're a bit of a wallflower. Nothing ventured, nothing gained.

Try not to sit on the fence as far as relationships are concerned between the 12th and the 15th. You have to make up your mind, even if indecision is crowding in on you. Take some firm action that involves self-sacrifice. In the end you'll be glad that you were true to yourself and made the break.

With Venus and Mercury providing you with excellent good-luck vibrations during December, your social life will be particularly busy. With Mars, Pluto and Venus in excellent aspect, your communication will be powerful and convincing. Mercury also moving in its forward motion means some of your decisions will be better informed; you will feel extremely confident and be received well.

There will be some exciting festivities in your home after the 21st and, with the new Moon of the 24th occurring in your financial zone, these two areas of your life will be intertwined. Getting ahead may be less important to you than showing affection to the ones you love and so make some concessions for them by not overworking this Christmas.

Because the new Moon occurs in your zone of income, many Scorpios will experience a job offer or an unexpected boost through a friend or loved one. Hey, Santa Claus does exist! There is some wonderful communication occurring around the 22nd that will open up some new doors to you through these social contacts.

Once again the influence of the Sun and Jupiter on your marital sector between the 23rd and the 30th is extremely important. It's an excellent omen with which to complete your year and it indicates that, when all is said and done, you should finish 2011 surrounded by goodwill, understanding and a little passion thrown in for good measure.

Work and money

The year 2011 finishes on an excellent note, with the new Moon in December highlighting grand opportunities to earn extra money and possibly even begin a new business venture. There will be many communications, especially between the 1st and 4th, due to the combined influence of the Sun and Mercury. However, hold off making a firm decision until the 14th, when Mercury is in forward motion.

You can make a great impression between the 15th and the 20th, so you shouldn't make yourself scarce when business and pleasure combine in office parties and other festive events leading up to Christmas. It's a perfect time of the year to network, hand your business cards around, and really set the pace for the coming year in terms of your professional activities.

Although you feel as if there are still some responsibilities to take care of, you'll feel more comfortable between the 20th and the 22nd and will be able to relax and enjoy what is on offer socially as well as professionally.

A stroke of good luck between the 23rd and the 29th is a perfect end to your financial and professional year.

Destiny dates

Positive: 7, 8, 9, 10, 16, 17, 18, 19, 20, 21, 22, 23, 24, 25, 26, 27, 28, 29, 30

Negative: None

Mixed: 2, 3, 4, 5, 6, 12, 13, 14, 15

2011:

Astronumerology

I think I've discovered the secret of life: You just hang around until you get used to it.

— Charles M. Schulz

The power behind your name

It's hard to believe that your name resonates with a numerical vibration, but it's true! By simply adding the numbers of your name, you can see which planet rules you and what effects your name will have on your life and destiny. According to the ancient Chaldean system of numerology, each number is assigned a planetary energy. Take a look at the chart below to see how each alphabetical letter is connected to a planetary energy:

AIQJY	=	1	**Sun**
BKR	=	2	**Moon**
CGLS	=	3	**Jupiter**
DMT	=	4	**Uranus**
EHNX	=	5	**Mercury**
UVW	=	6	**Venus**
OZ	=	7	**Neptune**
FP	=	8	**Saturn**
—	=	9	**Mars**

The number 9 is not allotted a letter because it is considered 'unknowable'. Once the numbers have been added, establish which single planet rules your name and personal affairs. At this point the number 9 can be used for interpretation. Do you think it's unusual that many famous actors, writers and musicians have modified their names? This is to attract luck and good fortune, which can be made easier by using the energies of a friendlier planet. Try experimenting with the table and see how new names affect you. It's so much fun, and you may even attract greater love, wealth and worldly success!

Look at the following example to work out the power of your name. A person named Andrew Brown would calculate his ruling planet by correlating each letter to a number in the table, like this:

A N D R E W B R O W N
1 5 4 2 5 6 2 2 7 6 5

Now add the numbers like this:

1 + 5 + 4 + 2 + 5 + 6 + 2 + 2 + 7 + 6 + 5 = 45

Then add 4 + 5 = 9

The ruling number of Andrew Brown's name is 9, which is ruled by Mars (see how the 9 can now be used?). Now study the name–number table to reveal the power of your name. The numbers 4 and 5 will also play a secondary role in Andrew's character and destiny, so in this case you would also study the effects of Uranus (4) and Mercury (5).

Name–number table

Your name-number	Ruling planet	Your name characteristics
1	Sun	Attractive personality. Magnetic charm. Superman-, superwoman-like vitality and physical energy. Incredibly active and gregarious. Enjoys outdoor activities and sports. Has friends and individuals in powerful positions. Good government connections. Intelligent, spectacular, flashy and successful. A loyal number for love and relationships.
2	Moon	Feminine and soft, emotional temperament. Fluctuating moods but intuitive, and possibly even clairvoyant abilities. Ingenious nature and kind-hearted expression of feelings. Loves family, mothering and home life. Night owl who probably needs more sleep. Success with the public and/or women generally.
3	Jupiter	Sociable, optimistic number with fortunate destiny. Attracts opportunities without too much effort. Great sense of timing. Religious or spiritual inclinations. Naturally drawn to investigate the meaning of life. Philosophical insight. Enjoys travel and to explore the world and different cultures.
4	Uranus	Volatile character with many peculiar aspects. Likes to experiment and test novel experiences. Forward thinking, with many extraordinary friends. Gets bored easily so needs plenty of inspiring activities. Pioneering, technological and creative. Wilful and obstinate at times. Unforeseen events in life may be positive or negative.

Your name-number	Ruling planet	Your name characteristics
5	Mercury	Sharp wit, quick thinking and with great powers of speech. Extremely active life. Always on the go, living on nervous energy. Youthful outlook and never grows old. Looks younger than actual age. Young friends and humorous disposition. Loves reading and writing. Great communicator.
6	Venus	Delightful and charming. Graceful and eye-catching personality who cherishes and nourishes friends. Very active social life. Musical or creative interests. Great moneymaking opportunities as well as numerous love affairs indicated. Career in the public eye is quite likely. Loves family but is often troubled over divided loyalties with friends.
7	Neptune	Intuitive, spiritual and self-sacrificing nature. Easily duped by those who need help. Loves to dream of life's possibilities. Has healing powers. Dreams are revealing and prophetic. Loves water and will have many journeys in life. Spiritual aspirations dominate worldly desires.
8	Saturn	Hard-working, ambitious person with slow yet certain achievements. Remarkable concentration and self-sacrifice for a chosen objective. Financially focused but generous when a person's trust is gained. Proficient in one's chosen field but is a hard taskmaster. Demands perfection and needs to relax and enjoy life.

Your name-number	Ruling planet	Your name characteristics
9	Mars	Extraordinary physical drive, desires and ambition. Sports and outdoor activities are major keys to health. Confrontational but likes to work and play really hard. Protects and defends family, friends and territory. Individual tastes in life but also self-absorbed. Needs to listen to others' advice to gain greater successes.

Your 2011 planetary ruler

Astrology and numerology are intimately connected. As already shown, each planet rules over a number between 1 and 9. Both your name *and* your birth date are governed by planetary energies.

Simply add the numbers of your birth date and the year in question to find out which planet will control the coming year for you. Here is an example:

If you were born on the 12th of November, add the numerals 1 and 2, for your day of birth, and 1 and 1, for your month of birth, to the year in question, in this case 2011, the current year, like this:

Add 1 + 2 + 1 + 1 + 2 + 0 + 1 + 1 = 9

The planet ruling your individual karma for 2011 will be Mars because this planet rules the number 9.

You can even take your ruling name-number, as shown previously, and add it to the year in question, to throw more light on your coming personal affairs, like this:

A N D R E W B R O W N = 9

Year coming = 2011

Add 9 + 2 + 0 + 1 + 1 = 13

Add 1 + 3 = 4

This is the ruling year number, using your name-number as a basis.

Therefore, study Uranus's (number 4) influence for 2011. Enjoy!

1 is the year of the Sun

Overview

The year 2011 is the commencement of a new cycle for you. Because the Sun rules the number 1, the dominant energy for you in the coming year is solar, which is also connected to the sign of Leo. Expect the coming year to be full of great accomplishments and a high reputation regarding new plans and projects. This is the turning of a new page in the book of your life.

You will experience an uplifting of your physical energies, which makes you ready to assume fresh responsibilities in a new nine-year cycle. Whatever you begin now will surely be successful.

Your physical vitality is strong and your health should improve. If you've been suffering physical ailments, this is the time to improve your physical wellbeing because recovery will be certain.

You're a magnetic person this year, so attracting people into your life won't be difficult. Expect a new circle of friends and possibly even new lovers coming into your life. Get ready to be invited to many parties and different engagements. However, don't go burning the midnight oil because this will overstretch your physical powers.

Don't be too cocky with friends or employers. Maintain some humility, which will make you even more popular throughout 2011.

Love and pleasure

Because this is the commencement of a new cycle, you'll be lucky in love. The Sun also has influence over children, so your family life will also entail more responsibility. Music, art and any other creative activities will be high on your agenda and may be the source of a new romance for you.

Work

Because you are so popular and powerful this year, you won't need to exert too much effort to attract luck, money and new windows of opportunity through your work and group activities. Changes that you make professionally now will pay off, particularly in the coming couple of years. Promotions are likely and don't be surprised to see some extra money coming your way as a pay rise.

Improving your luck

Because Leo and the number 1 are your rulers this year, you'll be especially lucky without too much effort. The months of July and August, being ruled by Leo, are very lucky for you. The 1st, 8th, 15th and 22nd hours of Sundays will be especially lucky. You may also find yourself meeting Leos and they may be able to contribute something to your good fortune throughout the coming year.

This year your lucky numbers are 1, 10, 19 and 28.

2 is the year of the Moon

Overview

The Moon represents emotional, nurturing, mothering and feminine aspects of our natures and 2011 will embody all of these traits in you, and more.

Groundbreaking opportunities in your relationships with family members can be expected. This will offer you immense satisfaction.

Your emotional and mental moods and habits should be examined. If you are reactive in your life, this year will be the perfect time to take greater control of yourself. The sign of Cancer, which is ruled by the Moon, is also very much linked to the number 2 and therefore people born under this sign may have an important role to play in your life.

Love and pleasure

Your home, family life and interpersonal relationships will be the main arenas of activity for you in 2011. You'll be able to take your relationships to a new level. If you haven't had the time to dedicate and devote yourself to the people you love, you can do so throughout the coming twelve months.

Thinking of moving? These lunar energies may cause you to change your residence or renovate your current home to make your living circumstances much more in tune with your mind and your heart.

Work

Working from home can be a great idea—or at least, spending more time alone to focus your attention on what you really want—will benefit you professionally. You need to control yourself and think carefully about how you are going to achieve your desired goals.

Women can be a source of opportunity for you and, if you're looking for a change in work, use your connections, especially feminine ones, to achieve success.

Improving your luck

The sign of Cancer being ruled by the Moon also has a connection with Mondays and therefore this will be one of your luckier days throughout 2011. The month of July is also one in which some of your dreams may come true. The 1st, 8th, 15th and 22nd hours on Mondays are successful times. Pay special attention to the new and full Moons in 2011.

The numbers 2, 11, 20, 29 and 38 are lucky for you.

3 is the year of Jupiter

Overview

Number 3 is one of the luckiest numbers, being ruled by Jupiter. Therefore, 2011 should be an exciting and expansive year for you. The planet Jupiter and the sign of Sagittarius will dominate the affairs of your life.

Under the number 3 you'll desire a richer, deeper and broader experience of life and as a result your horizons will also be much broader. You have the ability to gain money, to increase your popularity, and to have loads of fun.

Generosity is one of the key words of the number 3 and you're likely to help others fulfil their desires, too. There is an element of humanity and self-sacrifice indicated by this number and so the more spiritual and compassionate elements of your personality will bubble to the surface. You can improve yourself as a person generally, and this is also a year when your good karma should be used unselfishly to help others as well as yourself.

Love and pleasure

Exploring the world through travel will be an important component of your social and romantic life throughout 2011. It's quite likely that, through your travels and your contacts in other places, you may meet people who will spur you on to love and romance.

You'll be a bit of a gambler in 2011 and the number 3 will make you speculative. This could mean a few false starts in the area of love, but don't be afraid to explore the signs of human possibilities. You may just meet your soulmate as a result.

If you're currently in a relationship, you can deepen your love for each other and push the relationship to new heights.

Work

This is a fortunate year for you. The year 2011 brings you opportunities and success. Your employers will listen to your ideas and accommodate your requests for extra money.

Starting a new job is likely, possibly even your own business. You will try something big and bold. Have no fear: success is on your side.

Improving your luck

As long as you don't push yourself too hard you will have a successful year. Maintain a first-class plan and stick to it. Be realistic about what you are capable of. On the 1st, 8th, 15th and 24th hours of Thursdays, your intuition will make you lucky.

Your lucky numbers this year are 3, 12, 21 and 30. March and December are lucky months. The year 2011 will bring you some unexpected surprises.

4 is the year of Uranus
Overview

Expect the unexpected in 2011. This is a year when you achieve extraordinary things but have to make serious choices between several opportunities. You need to break free of your own past self-limitations, off-load any baggage that is hindering you, in both your personal and professional lives. It's an independent year and self-development will be important to achieving success.

Discipline is one of your key words for 2011. Maintain an orderly lifestyle, a clear-cut routine, and get more sleep. You'll gain strong momentum to fulfil yourself in each and every department of your life.

Love and pleasure

You may be dissatisfied with the current status quo in your relationships, so you're likely to break free and experiment with something different. Your relationships will be anything but dull or routine. You're looking for someone who is prepared to explore emotional and sexual landscapes.

Your social life will also be exciting and you'll meet unusual people who will open your eyes to new and fruitful activities. Spiritual and self-help activities will also capture your attention and enable you to make the most of your new friendships.

Work

The number 4 is modern, progressive and ruled by Uranus. Due to this, all sorts of technological gadgets, computing and Internet activities will play a significant role in your professional life. Move ahead with the times and upgrade your professional skills, because any new job you attempt will require it.

Work could be a little overwhelming, especially if you've not been accustomed to keeping a tight schedule. Be more efficient with your time.

Groups are important to your work efforts this year, so utilise your friends in finding a position you desire. Listen to their advice and become more of a team player because this will be a short cut in your pathway to success.

Improving your luck

Slow your pace this year because being impulsive will only cause you to make errors and waste time. 'Patience is a virtue', but in your case, when being ruled by the number 4, patience will be even more important for you.

The 1st, 8th, 15th and 20th hours of any Saturday will be very lucky for you in 2011.

Your lucky numbers are 4, 13, 22 and 31.

5 is the year of Mercury

Overview

Owing to the rulership of 2011 by the number 5, your intellectual and communicative abilities will be at a peak. Your imagination is also greatly stimulated by Mercury and so exciting new ideas will be constantly churning in your mind.

The downside of the number 5 is its convertible nature, which means it's likely that, when crunch times come and you have to make decisions, it will be difficult to do so. Get all your information together before drawing a firm conclusion. Develop a strong will and unshakable attitude to overcome distractions.

Contracts, new job offers and other agreements also need to be studied carefully before coming to any decision. Business skills and communication are the key words for your life in 2011.

Love and pleasure

One of the contributing factors to your love life in 2011 is service. You must learn to give to your partner if you wish to receive. There may be a change in your routine and this will be necessary if you are to keep your love life exciting, fresh and alive.

You could be critical, so be careful if you are trying to correct the behaviour of others. You'll be blunt and this will alienate you from your peers. Maintain some control over your critical mind before handing out your opinions.

You are likely to become interested in beautifying yourself and looking your best.

Work

Your ideas will be at the forefront of your professional activities this year. You are fast, capable and also innovative in the way you conduct yourself in the workplace. If you need to make any serious changes, however, it is best to think twice before 'jumping out of the pan and into the fire'.

Travel will also be a big component of your working life this year, and you can expect a hectic schedule with lots of flitting about here, there and everywhere. Pace yourself.

Improving your luck

Your greatest fortune will be in communicating ideas. Don't jump from one idea to another too quickly, though, because this will dilute your success.

Listen to your body signals as well because your health is strongly governed by the number 5. Sleep well, eat sensibly and exercise regularly to rebuild your resilience and strength.

The 1st, 8th, 15th and 20th hours of Wednesdays are your luckiest, so schedule your meetings and other important social engagements at these times.

Throughout 2011 your lucky numbers are 5, 14, 23 and 32.

6 is the year of Venus

Overview

The number 6 can be summed up in one beautiful four-letter word: LOVE! Venus rules 6 and is well known for its sensual, romantic and marital overtones. The year 2011 offers you all of this and more. If you're looking for a soulmate, it's likely to happen under a 6 vibration.

This year is a period of hard work to improve your security and finances. Saving money, cutting costs and looking to your future will be important. Keep in mind that this is a year of sharing love *and* material resources.

Love and pleasure

Romance is a key feature of 2011 and, if you're currently in a relationship, you can expect it to become more fulfilling. Important karmic connections are likely during this 6 year for those of you who are not yet married or in a relationship.

Beautify yourself, get a new hairstyle, work on looking your best through improving your fashion sense, new styles of jewellery and getting out there and showing the world what you're made of. This is a year in which your social engagements result in better relationships.

Try not to overdo it, because Venus has a tendency towards excess. Moderation in all things is important in a Venus year 6.

Work

The year 2011 will stimulate your knowledge about finance and your future security. You'll be capable of cutting back expenses and learning how to stretch a dollar. There could be surplus cash this year, increased income or some additional bonuses. You'll use this money to improve your living circumstances because home life is also important under a 6 year.

Your domestic situation could also be tied in with your work. During this year of Venus, your business and social activities will overlap.

Improving your luck

Money will flow as long as you keep an open mind and positive attitude. Remove negative personality traits obstructing you from greater luck. Be moderate in your actions and don't focus primarily on money. Your spiritual needs also require attention.

The 1st, 8th, 15th and 20th hours on Fridays are extremely lucky for you this year and new opportunities can arise when you least expect it.

The numbers 6, 15, 24 and 33 will generally increase your luck.

7 is the year of Neptune

Overview

Under a 7 year of Neptune, your spiritual and intuitive powers peak. Although your ideals seem clearer and more spiritually orientated, others may not understand your purpose. Develop the power of your convictions to balance your inner ideals with the practical demands of life.

You must learn to let go of your past emotional issues, break through these barriers to improve your life and your relationships this year. This might require you to sever ties with some of the usual people you have become accustomed to being with, which will give you the chance to focus on your own inner needs.

Love and pleasure

Relationships may be demanding and it's at this point in your life that you'll realise you have to give something to yourself as well, not just give to others indefinitely. If the people that matter most in your life are not reciprocating and meeting your needs, you'll have to make some important changes this year.

When it comes to helping others, pick your mark. Not everyone is deserving of the love and resources you have to offer. If you're indiscriminate, you could find yourself with egg on your face if you have been taken advantage of. Be firm, but compassionate.

Work

Compassionate work best describes 2011 under a 7 year. But the challenges of your professional life give you greater insight into yourself and the ability to see clearly what you *don't* want in your life any more. Remove what is unnecessary and this will pave the way for brighter successes.

Caring for and helping others will be important because your work will now bring you to a point where you realise that selfishness, money and security are not the only important things in life. Helping others will be part of your process, which will bring excellent benefits.

Improving your luck

Self-sacrifice, along with discipline and personal discrimination, bring luck. Don't let people use you because this will only result in more emotional baggage. The law of karma states that what you give, you will receive in greater measure; but sometimes the more you give, the more people take, too. Remember that.

The 1st, 8th, 15th and 20th hours of Tuesdays will be lucky times this year.

Try the numbers 7, 16, 25 and 34 to increase your luck.

8 is the year of Saturn

Overview

The number 8 is the most practical of the numbers, being ruled by Saturn and Capricorn. This means that your discipline, attention to detail and hard work will help you achieve your goals. Remaining solitary and not being overly involved with people will help you focus on things that matter. Resisting temptation will be part of your challenge this year, but doing so will also help you become a better person.

Love and pleasure

Balance your personal affairs with work. If you pay too much attention to your work, finances and your professional esteem, you may be missing out on the simple things in life, mainly love and affection.

Being responsible is certainly a great way to show your love to the ones who matter to you, such as your family members. But if you're concerned only with work and no play, it makes for a very dull family life. Make a little more time to enjoy your family and friends and schedule some time off on the weekends so you can enjoy the journey, not just the goal.

Work

You can make a lot of money this year and, if you've been focused on your work for the last couple of years, this is a time when money should flow to you. The Chinese believe the number 8 is indeed the money number and can bring you the fruits of your hard labour.

Because you're cautious and resourceful you'll be able to save more this year, but try not to be too stingy with your money.

Under an 8 year you'll take on new responsibilities. You mustn't do this for the sake of looking good. If you truly like the work that is being offered, by all means take it. But if it's simply for the sake of ego, you'll be very disappointed.

Improving your luck

This year you could be a little reluctant to try new things. But if you are overly cautious, you may miss opportunities. Don't act impulsively on what is being offered, of course, but do be open to trying some alternative things as well.

Be gentle and kind to yourself. By pampering yourself you send out a strong signal to the universe that you are deserving of some rewards.

The 1st, 8th, 15th and 20th hours of Saturdays are the best times for you in 2011.

The numbers 1, 8, 17, 26 and 35 are your lucky numbers.

9 is the year of Mars

Overview

The year 2011 is the final year of a nine-year cycle and this will be dominated by Aries and Mars. You'll be rushing madly to complete many things, so be careful not to overstep the mark of your capability. Work hard but balance your life with adequate rest.

In your relationships you will realise that you are at odds with your partner and want different things. This is the time to talk it out. If the communication between you isn't flowing well, you might find yourself leaving the relationship and moving on to bigger or better things. Worthwhile communication is a two-way street that will benefit both of you.

Love and pleasure

Mars is very pushy and infuses the number 9 with this kind of energy. The upshot is you need to be gentle in conveying your ideas and offering your views. Avoid arguments if you want to improve your relationships.

If you feel it's time for a change, discuss it with your partner. You can work through this feeling together and create an exciting new pathway for your love life. Don't get too angry with the little things in life. Get out and play some sport if you feel you are inappropriately taking out your bad moods on the ones you love.

Work

You have an intense drive and strong capability to achieve anything you choose in 2011. But be careful you don't overdo things, because you are prone to pushing yourself too far. Pace your deadlines, stagger the workload and, if possible, delegate some of the more menial tasks to others so you'll have time to do your own work properly.

Number 9 has an element of leadership associated with it, so you may be asked to take over and lead the group. This brings with it added responsibility but can also inspire you greatly.

Improving your luck

Restlessness is one of the problems that the number 9 brings with it, so you must learn to meditate and pacify your mind so you can take advantage of what the universe has to offer. If you're scattered in your energies, your attention will miss vital opportunities and your relationships could also become rather problematic as well.

Your health and vitality will remain strong as long as you rest adequately and find suitable outlets for your tension.

The 1st, 8th, 15th and 20th hours of Tuesdays will be lucky for you throughout 2011. Your lucky numbers are 9, 18, 27 and 36.

SCORPIO

2011:
Your Daily Planner

The significant problems we face cannot be resolved at the same level of thinking we were at when we created them.

— Albert Einstein

There is a little-known branch of astrology called electional astrology, and it can help you select the most appropriate times for many of your day-to-day activities.

Ancient astrologers understood the planetary patterns and how they impacted on each of us. This allowed them to suggest the best possible times to start various important activities. Many farmers today still use this approach: they understand the phases of the Moon, and attest to the fact that planting seeds on certain lunar days produces a far better crop than planting on other days.

The following section covers many areas of day-to-day life, and uses the cycles of the Moon and the combined strength of the other planets to work out the best times to start different types of activity.

So to create your own personal almanac, first select the activity you are interested in, then quickly scan the year for the best months to start it. When you have selected the month, you can finetune your timing by finding the best specific dates. You can then be sure that the planetary energies will be in sync with you, offering you the best possible outcome.

Coupled with what you know about your monthly and weekly trends, the daily planner can be a powerful tool to help you capitalise on opportunities that come your way this year.

Good luck, and may the planets bless you with great success, fortune and happiness in 2011!

Starting activities

How many times have you made a new year's resolution to begin a diet or be a better person in your relationships? And how many times has it not worked out? Well, part of the reason may be that you started out at the wrong time, because how successful you are is strongly influenced by the position of the Moon and the planets when you begin a particular activity. You will be more successful with the following endeavours if you start them on the days indicated.

Relationships

We all feel more empowered on some days than on others. This is because the planets have some power over us—their movement and their relationships to each other determine the ebb and flow of our energies. And our level of self-confidence and our sense of romantic magnetism play an important part in the way we behave in relationships.

Your daily planner tells you the ideal dates for meeting new friends, initiating a love affair, spending time with family and loved ones—it even tells you the most appropriate times for sexual encounters.

You'll be surprised at how much more impact you can make in your relationships when you tune yourself in to the planetary energies on these special dates.

Falling in love or restoring love

During these times you could expect favourable energies to be present to meet your soulmate. Or, if you've had difficulty in a relationship, you can approach the one you love to rekindle both your and their emotional responses.

January	8, 9, 10, 13, 14, 15, 18, 19, 20, 21
February	4, 5, 6, 9, 10, 11, 14
March	1, 9, 10, 14, 15, 16, 17
April	5, 6, 17, 25, 26
May	3, 4, 6, 7, 8, 9, 10, 11, 14, 15, 22, 23, 24
June	1, 11, 18, 19, 20, 28, 29, 30
July	7, 8, 26, 27, 30, 31
August	3, 12, 13, 14, 22, 23, 27, 31
September	1, 18, 19, 20, 26, 27, 28, 29, 30
October	12, 13, 17, 18, 25, 26, 29, 30, 31
November	2, 3, 4, 5, 6, 9, 17, 29
December	3, 7, 8, 11, 14, 15, 18, 19, 29, 30

Special times with friends and family

Socialising, partying and having a good time with those you enjoy being with is highly favourable under the following dates. These are also excellent days to spend time with family and loved ones in a domestic environment:

January	17, 20, 21
February	2, 9, 10, 11, 18, 19, 20, 21, 22, 23, 24, 28
March	1, 11, 14, 16, 17, 20
April	2, 11, 12, 21, 22, 26
May	6, 9, 10, 11, 14, 15, 22, 23, 24
June	4, 8, 10, 12, 19, 20, 25, 26, 28
July	7, 8, 16, 23, 30, 31
August	4, 5, 6, 7, 13, 20, 27, 31
September	1, 6, 18, 19, 20, 29, 30
October	1, 16, 17, 25, 26
November	2, 12, 13, 17, 26, 29
December	11, 14, 15, 18, 19, 27, 28

Healing or resuming a relationship

If you're trying to get back together with the one you love and need a heart-to-heart or deep and meaningful conversation, you can try the following dates to do so:

January	2, 3, 4, 5, 6, 7, 8, 9, 10, 11, 12, 13, 14, 15, 16, 17, 18, 19, 20, 21, 28

February	1, 2, 4, 5, 6, 7, 21, 22, 23, 24, 28
March	1, 8, 9, 10, 11, 14, 16, 17, 18, 19, 20
April	2, 11, 12, 26
May	1, 6, 7, 8, 9, 10, 11, 12, 13, 15, 19, 22, 24, 25, 26, 27, 28
June	5, 12, 14, 15, 16, 19, 23, 25, 26, 27, 28, 29, 30
July	4, 6, 7, 8, 9, 10, 16, 19, 21, 23, 28, 29, 30, 31
August	1, 2, 3, 13, 15, 16, 20, 27, 29, 30, 31
September	1, 2, 3, 4, 5, 6, 13, 15, 16, 17, 18, 19, 20, 21, 22, 23, 25, 28, 29
October	12, 13, 15, 16, 17, 18, 25, 27, 29
November	2, 4, 5, 6, 15, 16, 17, 26, 29
December	11, 19, 20, 21, 22, 23

Sexual encounters

Physical and sexual energies are well favoured on the following dates. The energies of the planets enhance your moments of intimacy during these times:

January	2, 3, 4, 5, 6, 7, 8, 9, 10, 11, 12, 20, 21, 25
February	7, 8, 18, 19, 20, 21
March	1, 8, 11, 14, 20, 21

April	4, 11, 12, 25, 26, 27, 28, 29
May	2, 9, 10, 11, 14, 15, 22, 23, 24
June	1, 11, 12, 18, 19, 20, 28, 29, 30
July	7, 8, 16, 19, 20, 21, 23, 30
August	3, 12, 13, 14, 20, 22, 27, 31
September	1, 18, 19, 20, 29, 30
October	1, 13, 15, 18, 19, 20, 21, 22, 25, 26
November	2, 3, 11, 15, 16, 17, 18, 21, 22
December	5, 6, 12, 13, 14, 15, 18, 19

Health and wellbeing

Your aura and life force are susceptible to the movements of the planets; in particular, they respond to the phases of the Moon.

The following dates are the most appropriate times to begin a diet, have cosmetic surgery, or seek medical advice. They also tell you when the best times are to help others.

Feeling of wellbeing

Your physical as well as your mental alertness should be strong on these following dates. You can plan your activities and expect a good response from others:

January	7, 9, 10, 11, 12, 13, 14, 18, 20, 21
February	4, 18, 19, 20, 21, 22, 23, 24
March	16, 17, 19, 20
April	2, 7, 12, 20, 22, 25, 26
May	9, 10, 11, 14, 15, 16, 17, 22, 24, 25
June	4, 8, 10, 11, 12, 16, 17, 18, 19, 20, 21, 23, 25, 26
July	7, 8, 9, 10, 26, 27, 30
August	3, 4, 5, 6, 12, 13, 14, 17, 19, 22, 27, 31
September	1, 13, 26, 27, 28, 29, 30
October	1, 16, 17, 25, 26, 30, 31
November	1, 2, 3, 4, 5, 6, 17, 29
December	4, 11, 14, 15, 18, 19, 21, 22, 23, 30

Healing and medical

These times are good for approaching others who have expertise when you need some deeper understanding. They are also favourable for any sort of healing or medication, and for making appointments with doctors or psychologists. Planning surgery around these dates should bring good results.

Often giving up our time and energy to assist others doesn't necessarily result in the expected outcome. By lending a helping hand to a friend on the following dates, the results should be favourable:

January	1, 2, 3, 4, 5, 6, 7, 8, 14, 15, 16, 17, 18, 19, 20, 21, 22, 23, 24, 25, 26, 27, 28, 29, 31
February	3, 4, 5, 6, 7, 8, 9, 10, 13, 15, 16, 17, 18, 19, 21, 22, 23, 24, 25, 26, 27
March	4, 9, 10, 11, 12, 15, 16
April	2, 9, 10, 11, 12, 13, 14, 15, 16, 17, 18, 19, 20, 21, 22, 23, 24, 25, 26, 27, 28, 29, 30
May	1, 2, 3, 4, 5, 6, 8, 9, 10, 11, 12, 13, 14, 15, 16, 17, 18, 19, 20, 21, 22, 23, 24, 25, 30
June	23, 26, 28
July	3, 10, 11, 12
August	7, 8, 9, 10, 11, 12, 13, 14, 15, 16, 20, 21, 25
September	23, 25, 26, 27
October	20, 21, 22, 23, 24, 25, 26, 27, 28, 29, 30, 31
November	1, 2, 3, 4, 5, 6, 7, 8, 9, 10, 11, 12, 13, 14, 15, 16, 17, 18, 19, 20, 21, 22, 23, 24, 25, 30
December	1, 2, 3, 4, 5, 6, 7, 8, 9, 10, 30

Money

Money is an important part of life, and involves lots of decisions—decisions about borrowing, investing, spending. The ideal times for transactions are very much influenced by the planets, and whether your investment or nest egg grows or doesn't grow can often be linked to timing. Making your decisions on the following dates could give you a whole new perspective on your financial future:

Managing wealth and money

To build your nest egg it's a good time to open a bank account and invest money on the following dates:

January	2, 3, 9, 10, 11, 12, 13, 14, 15, 16, 17, 18, 19, 20, 21, 22, 24, 28
February	3, 4, 5, 6, 7, 8, 9, 11, 13, 14, 16, 18, 19, 20, 21, 22, 23, 24, 25, 26, 27
March	4, 8, 11, 12, 13, 14, 16, 17, 18, 19
April	2, 7, 8, 9, 10, 11, 12, 13, 16, 17, 18, 19, 20, 21, 22, 23, 24, 25
May	1, 6, 7, 8, 9, 10, 11, 12, 13, 14, 15, 16, 17, 18, 19, 20, 21, 22, 23, 24, 25, 30
June	3, 4, 5, 8, 16, 17, 18, 19, 20, 23, 25, 26, 27, 28
July	4, 5, 6, 7, 8, 9, 10, 11, 12, 16, 23, 25, 28, 29, 30, 31
August	1, 2, 3, 4, 5, 6, 7, 8, 9, 10, 11, 12, 13, 14, 15, 16, 17, 19, 20, 30, 31
September	2, 11, 13, 15, 23, 25, 26, 27, 28, 29, 30

October	1, 2, 3, 4, 5, 6, 7, 8, 13, 14, 15, 16, 17, 18, 19, 21, 24, 25, 26, 27, 28, 29, 30, 31
November	2, 3, 4, 5, 6, 7, 9, 11, 12, 13, 14, 15, 16, 17, 18, 19, 20, 23, 25, 29
December	6, 13, 19, 26, 31

Spending

It's always fun to spend, but the following dates are more in tune with this activity and are likely to give you better results:

January	8, 9, 10, 11, 12, 13, 14, 15
February	9, 11, 18, 19
March	9
April	22
May	6, 7, 8, 9, 10, 11, 12, 13, 14, 17, 18, 19, 20, 21, 22, 23, 24
June	4, 8, 10, 11, 12, 14, 16, 17, 19
July	6, 7, 8, 9, 10, 11, 31
August	1, 2, 3, 4, 5, 6, 15, 16, 17, 18, 19, 30, 31
September	1, 2, 3, 4, 17, 19, 28, 29, 30
October	12, 13, 14, 15, 16, 17, 18, 19, 27, 28, 29, 30, 31
November	2, 3, 4, 5, 6, 7
December	3, 4, 5, 22, 23

Selling

If you're thinking of selling something, whether it is small or large, consider the following dates as ideal times to do so:

January	2, 3, 9, 10, 11, 12, 13, 14, 15, 16, 17, 18, 19, 20, 22, 24, 28
February	3, 4, 5, 6, 7, 8, 9, 11, 13, 14, 16, 18, 19, 20, 21, 22, 23, 24, 25, 26, 27
March	4, 8, 11, 12, 13, 14, 16, 17, 18, 19
April	2, 7, 8, 9, 10, 11, 12, 13, 16, 17, 18, 19, 20, 21, 22, 23, 24
May	1, 6, 7, 8, 9, 10, 11, 12, 13, 14, 15, 16, 17, 18, 19, 20, 21, 22, 23, 24, 25, 26, 30
June	3, 4, 5, 8, 16, 17, 18, 19, 20, 23, 25, 26, 27, 28
July	4, 5, 6, 7, 8, 9, 10, 11, 12, 16, 23, 25, 28, 29, 30, 31
August	1, 2, 3, 4, 5, 6, 7, 8, 9, 10, 11, 12, 13, 14, 15, 16, 17, 19, 20, 30, 31
September	2, 11, 13, 15, 23, 25, 26, 27, 28, 29, 30
October	1, 2, 3, 4, 5, 6, 7, 8, 13, 14, 15, 16, 17, 18, 19, 21, 24, 25, 26, 27, 28, 29, 30, 31
November	2, 3, 4, 5, 6, 7, 9, 11, 12, 13, 14, 15, 16, 17, 18, 19, 20, 23, 25, 29
December	2, 3, 4, 5, 6, 7, 11, 30

Borrowing

Few of us like to borrow money, but if you must, taking out a loan on the following dates will be positive:

January	1, 20, 21, 26, 27, 28, 31
February	1, 2, 22, 23, 24
March	1, 22, 23, 26, 27, 29, 31
April	1, 18, 19, 22, 23, 24, 25, 26, 27, 28, 29
May	17, 18, 19, 20, 21, 22, 23, 24, 25, 26
June	16, 17, 18, 19, 22
July	15, 16, 28, 29, 30
August	15, 16, 24, 25, 26, 27, 28
September	21, 22
October	21
November	14, 15, 16, 17, 23, 24
December	12, 13, 14, 15, 20, 21, 22, 23, 24

Speculation and investment

To invest your money and get a good return on that investment try taking a punt on the following dates:

January	3, 4, 5, 11, 12, 18, 19, 24, 25, 31
February	1, 7, 8, 14, 15, 20, 21, 27, 28
March	6, 7, 8, 14, 15, 20, 21, 26, 27

April	2, 3, 4, 10, 11, 16, 17, 22, 23, 24, 30
May	1, 7, 8, 14, 15, 20, 21, 27, 28, 29
June	3, 4, 5, 10, 11, 16, 17, 23, 24, 25
July	1, 2, 7, 8, 14, 15, 21, 22, 28, 29
August	3, 4, 10, 11, 17, 18, 19, 24, 25, 26, 31
September	1, 6, 7, 13, 14, 15, 21, 22, 27, 28
October	3, 4, 5, 11, 12, 18, 19, 25, 26, 31
November	1, 7, 8, 14, 15, 16, 21, 22, 27, 28
December	4, 5, 6, 12, 13, 18, 19, 25, 26, 31

Work and education

Your career is important to you, and continual improvement of your skills is therefore also crucial, professionally, mentally and socially. These dates will help you find out the most appropriate times to improve your professional talents and commence new work or education associated with your work.

You may need to decide when to start learning a new skill, when to ask for a promotion, and even when to make an important career change. Here are the days when your mental and educational power is strong.

Learning new skills

Educational pursuits are lucky and bring good results on the following dates:

January · 16, 17

February	12, 13
March	11, 12, 13, 18, 19
April	7, 8, 9, 14, 15
May	5, 6, 12, 13
June	2, 8, 9, 14, 15
July	5, 6, 11, 12, 13
August	1, 2, 8, 9, 29, 30
September	4, 5
October	1, 2, 29, 30
November	25, 26
December	9, 10

Changing career path or profession

If you're feeling stuck and need to move into a new professional activity, changing jobs is recommended at these times:

January	4, 5, 13, 14, 15
February	9, 10, 11
March	1, 2, 3, 9, 10, 11, 12, 18, 19, 20, 21
April	5, 6, 7, 8, 9, 14, 15, 16, 17, 25, 26
May	3, 4, 12, 13, 22, 23, 24
June	1, 2, 8, 9, 18, 19, 20, 28, 29, 30
July	5, 6, 14, 26, 27
August	3, 4, 10, 11, 22, 23, 29, 30, 31

September	1, 6, 7, 8, 9, 10, 18, 19, 20, 27, 28
October	3, 4, 5, 16, 17, 25, 26, 31
November	1, 2, 3, 9, 10, 29, 30
December	1, 7, 8, 9, 10, 11, 18, 19, 25, 26, 27, 28

Promotion, professional focus and hard work

To increase your mental focus and achieve good results from the work you do; promotions are also likely on the dates that follow:

January	3, 9, 10, 11, 12, 13, 14, 18
February	22, 23, 24, 25, 26, 27, 28
March	8, 10, 11, 13, 14, 16, 17, 18, 19
April	11, 12
May	6, 7, 8, 9, 10, 11, 12, 13, 15, 16, 17, 19, 21, 22, 23, 24
June	4, 5, 8, 11, 12, 14, 15, 16, 17, 19
July	16, 18, 19, 20, 23, 24, 25, 28, 29, 30
August	1, 2, 14, 15, 16, 17, 19, 30
September	1, 2, 3, 4, 5, 6, 11, 13, 16, 17, 19
October	13, 15, 16, 17, 18, 19
November	2, 4, 5, 6, 7, 12
December	25, 26

Travel

Setting out on a holiday or adventurous journey is exciting. Here are the most favourable times for doing this. Travel on the following dates is likely to give you a sense of fulfilment:

January	9, 10, 11, 12, 16, 17, 18, 19
February	4, 5, 6, 7, 15
March	19
April	7, 8, 9, 10, 11
May	15
June	4, 8, 10, 11
July	1, 5, 6
August	1, 2, 3, 4, 8
September	27, 28
October	1, 3, 4, 29, 30, 31
November	1, 4, 5, 6
December	3, 4, 5, 25, 29, 30

Beauty and grooming

Believe it or not, cutting your hair or nails has a powerful effect on your body's electromagnetic energy. If you cut your hair or nails at the wrong time of the month, you can reduce your level of vitality significantly. Use these dates to ensure you optimise your energy levels by staying in tune with the stars:

Haircuts

January	1, 2, 8, 9, 10, 16, 17, 28, 29, 30
February	25, 26
March	4, 5, 11, 12, 13, 14, 25, 31
April	1, 7, 8, 9, 20, 21, 27, 28, 29
May	5, 6, 18, 19, 25, 26
June	1, 2, 14, 15, 21, 22, 28, 29, 30
July	11, 12, 13, 18, 19, 20, 26, 27
August	8, 9, 15, 16, 22, 23
September	4, 5, 11, 12, 18, 19, 20
October	1, 2, 8, 9, 10, 16, 17, 29, 30
November	4, 5, 6, 12, 13, 25, 26
December	2, 3, 9, 10, 11, 23, 24, 29, 30

Cutting nails

January	11, 12, 13, 14, 15, 18, 19, 20, 21
February	7, 8, 9, 10, 11, 14, 16
March	6, 8, 9, 10, 14, 15
April	2, 3, 5, 6
May	4, 7, 8, 9, 10, 11, 27, 28, 29, 30, 31
June	3, 4, 5, 6, 7, 23, 25, 26, 27
July	1, 2, 3, 21, 22, 23, 24, 25, 28, 29, 30, 31

August	17, 19, 20, 24, 25, 26
September	13, 16, 17, 21, 22, 23, 24
October	11, 13, 15, 18, 19, 20, 21, 22
November	15, 16, 17, 18
December	4, 5, 6, 7, 8

Therapies, massage and self-pampering

January	1, 2, 8, 9, 10, 16, 17, 28, 29, 30
February	5, 6, 12, 13, 25, 26
March	4, 5, 11, 12, 13, 24, 25, 31
April	1, 7, 8, 9, 20, 21, 27, 28, 29
May	5, 6, 18, 19, 25, 26
June	1, 2, 14, 15, 21, 22, 28, 29, 30
July	11, 12, 13, 18, 19, 20, 26, 27
August	8, 9, 15, 16, 22, 23
September	4, 5, 11, 12, 18, 19, 20
October	1, 2, 8, 9, 10, 16, 17, 29, 30
November	4, 5, 6, 12, 13, 25, 26
December	2, 3, 9, 10, 11, 23, 24, 29, 30